Urban Poverty in the Caribbean

French Martinique as a Social Laboratory

Michel S. Laguerre

Associate Professor of Social Anthropology
University of California, Berkeley

St. Martin's Press　　New York

© Michel S. Laguerre 1990

First published in the United States of America in 1990

Printed in Great Britain

ISBN 0–312–04495–X

Library of Congress Cataloging-in-Publication Data

Laguerre, Michel S.
    Urban poverty in the Caribbean: the Martinican experience /
Michel S. Laguerre.
        p.   cm.
    Includes bibliographical references.
    ISBN 0–312–04495–X
    1. Urban poor—Martinique.   I. Title.
HV4065.9.A5L34   1990
305.5′69′0972982091732—dc20   89–77908
                                                   CIP

For my niece and nephews Freda, Serge,
Donald and Rodini

Contents

List of Figures and Maps

List of Tables

Introduction

The study of the contemporary Caribbean city allows us an opportunity to focus on a series of local and national problems that need to be tackled to understand the integration of the islands in the world system. The flow of processes, systems, structures and interactions that emerge in the city cannot be explained solely by focusing on the city as an isolated unit, but rather as the product of its relationships with the hinterland and the world at large. On the one hand, the city is the locus where these two external entities meet and influence the urban processual outcome. On the other hand, because of the urban influence in the shaping of the national space, the urban question becomes the privileged angle from which to understand parts and parcels of the national question.

The Caribbean city is by all evidence a microcosm of the country. The national structure of inequality finds its myriad expressions in the urban environment. Not only does the city provide the ideological back-up – as the locus where élite ideologies are produced and reproduced – but also the men and women who occupy the positions that sustain the inequality structure. The city serves then as an arena where inequality and poverty are daily manufactured. Moreover, what one learns here on the articulation of urban poverty can shed a great deal of light on the causes of rural poverty as well.

Since the second world war, with the decrease in importance of the agricultural sector in most of the Caribbean islands, the primate city has emerged as a strategic pole of the economy. It is here that the policies concerning rural development are made, more often than not for the benefit of the urban élite, and it is here also that industrial production reaches its highest peak. By and large, agricultural production is oriented toward urban consumption and for urban transactions. Seen from this angle, one may venture to say that rural poverty has urban roots because the urban commercial and political élite decide on the prices of goods and serve as the main market for the rural population.

In this book Martinique is used as a social laboratory to investigate the process of reproduction of urban poverty in the Caribbean. The bulk of the data presented here concerns that island. When reliable data on the other present or former French, Spanish, British and Dutch islands are available, they are compared or contrasted with the

Martinican situation. This procedure is necessary to show that the mechanisms that sustain the reproduction of urban poverty are not peculiar to that island, but can also be found elsewhere in the Caribbean.

In effect what becomes clear from that level of analysis is the importance of the linkages of the primate city not only with the rural sector, but also with western Europe and North America. It is so because of structural factors including the three-way migration movement that characterises the Caribbean islands. Rural folks migrate to the city in search of employment; urban residents migrate to North America or to Europe to better their lives; and Caribbean immigrants living abroad return to their home islands mainly for economic purposes or retirement. The search for employment moves people then in both directions. It also transforms the Caribbean family into a multinational organisation with a headquarters in the home island and a subsidiary abroad, to use the vocabulary of the firm.

Deciphering the reproduction of the structure of urban poverty means also that one must pay attention to the urban space which serves as an infrastructural basis. The deconstruction of the urban space leads to the identification of macro-niches (slums and squatters' settlements) and micro-niches (yards) of poverty. Although the articulation of the poor neighbourhoods with the rest of the city may take various forms, what remains constant are the asymmetrical relations between the dominant sector and the poor sector. This is why I venture to study the process of the reproduction of urban poverty in the Caribbean here from the angle of the reproduction of asymmetrical relations.

Since I began the research for the book, several people have helped in many different ways. I am particularly grateful to Brigitte Rocher, Françoise Pereira, Nancy Rubin, Karen Platt, Betsy Amster, Maria Ward, Trudi Howell, Barbara Riley, Robert Miglian, Richard Tooker, Keith Lester and Mark Hall; all of them served as volunteers in the University of California Research Expeditions to Martinique during the Summer of 1985. They spent a few weeks in the field assisting me in whatever manners they could through interviewing people, drawing maps, and participating in group discussions. Mr and Mrs René Rocher provided us with hospitality in their home in Rivière L'Or. Louis Suivant, the energetic director of the Office of Urban Planning (ADUAM), allowed me to use the facilities in Fort-de-France as the headquarters of the project. Serge Letchimy and Max Tanic who had written their doctoral theses on Fort-de-France were also very helpful in discussing the issues with me and in helping with bibliographic resources. I am grateful to Anne Hublin and particularly to Roger Sanjek who commented on Chapter 4. Barbara Korta helped to calculate the interest gained or lost by informants who participated in informal savings associations and Jill Sellers provided me with editorial assistance. I want to thank my secretary Elmirie Robinson for typing the manuscript and Linh Do and Susan Lee for preparing the illustrations. The project was sponsored and financed by the University of California Research Expeditions Program. Two faculty grants awarded to me by the Committee on Research of the University of California at Berkeley allowed me to prepare the final draft of the manuscript for publication.

The content of the book was presented and discussed in several different places and before diverse audiences which greatly helped me to clarify my thoughts on some of the issues. One of the two initial interviews summarising the theoretical orientation of the book was aired on KTVU Channel 2 (Oakland, California) and the other was published in the *Oakland Tribune* in the spring of 1985. Two substantive interviews were also published in the columns of *France-Antilles* during the summer of 1985 for the benefit of the readers in Martinique, Guadeloupe, French Guyana and mainland France. Chapter 4 was read at the annual meetings of the American Anthropological Association held in the fall of 1985 in Washington DC. Chapter 3 was presented in the spring of 1986 at the Institute for the Study of Social Change of the University of California at Berkeley. Chapter 6 was prepared for the annual meetings of the Caribbean Studies Association held in Guadeloupe in the spring of 1988. Finally Chapter 2 was delivered at the annual meetings of the American Anthropological Association held in Phoenix, Arizona, in the fall of 1988. The book has also benefited from various exchanges I had with undergraduate, graduate and post-doctoral students who took my spring upper-division seminar on Primate Caribbean Cities.

The book studies the urban system from below. It pertains to explain it through an analysis of the reproduction of poverty. It connects the poor to the élite or, better, the structure of oppression to that of domination. In the process it reveals the role and structural position of the primate city in the integration of the national territory.

1 Urban Poverty and Social Reproduction

The theme of urban poverty that is addressed in this book will be illustrated by the existence and visibility of the phenomenon in one of the major cities of the Caribbean, namely, Fort-de-France, Martinique. Urban poverty in Martinique is a by-product of the plantation economy and the continuing dependence of the island on metropolitan France. It is not of recent origins; however, it has become a pronounced and shocking reality in the slums of Fort-de-France and other capitals of the Caribbean islands since the end of the Second World War.

During the colonial era there were indeed countless poor whites and blacks at the very bottom of the urban social structure. The whites were indentured servants and individuals who through some misfortune and the structural inequality of the functioning slave system were unable to do well in the colony. Among the urban blacks one found domestic slaves and free persons of colour – those who had recently purchased their freedom and those who were victims of the cyclical contraction of the labour market. Evidently there were also *cimarrones urbanos* (urban maroons) who formed a sizeable population in the city of Havana, Cuba, for example. These were slaves who escaped from their masters' domains and took refuge or lost themselves among the black population in marginal neighbourhoods of Havana.[1] In Santo Domingo, the Dominican Republic, and in San Juan, Puerto Rico, poor blacks participated in religious associations or brotherhoods similar to, for example, *la Cofradia de la Concepcion de Nuestra Señora*.[2] In San Juan mulatto dancers were even allowed to perform their *baile de espadas* (sword dance) as parts of the Corpus Christi celebrations (Mathews' 1980, p. 161). While in Nassau, in the Bahamas, they had developed their own neighbourhood, known today as 'Over-the-Hill',[3] in cities such as Charlotte Amalie, St Thomas, and Fredericksted and Christiansted, St Croix, free blacks and slaves provided a series of services: they were vendors of food, grass suppliers, carpenters, seamen. Their labour constituted the lifeblood of the local urban economy.[4] In Martinique, the presence of poor blacks was more apparent in Saint Pierre, where the most important commercial transactions took place, than in the administrative city of

Fort-de-France. Indeed Elizabeth (1977, p. 4) notes that from 1780 on, a true black urban proletariat became highly visible in Saint Pierre. One could seldom distinguish it from the population of slaves who were hired on a daily basis by people other than their masters, and who evidently shared whatever money they made with their owners. The revolutionary troubles that occurred in the town both in 1789 and in 1831 were sustained partly by the participation of these two groups of black urbanites (Elizabeth, 1977, p. 4).

Throughout the entire colonial era slavery was the main cause of poverty among city blacks. Slavery prevented them from holding positions of power as well as from being able to compete in the free market. In structural terms they were kept at the bottom of colonial society: they were not paid for their labour and were discriminated against in all avenues of power. The colonial system, through its legal apparatus, manufactured and reproduced poverty in the structural, not necessarily the physical, margins of the cities so as to be able to exploit the slave labour force. Poverty had a social function in colonial society. It was the inevitable result of a system of inequality engineered to benefit and maintain the dominant European group. The reproduction of the dominant class was dependent on the reproduction of the slave sector, which was forced, by legal and by physical means, to provide free labour to the white group. The reproduction of the slave group was similarly dependent on the reproduction of the dominant class, which was able to augment and enrich itself through the economic exploitation of the slaves.

The reproduction of poverty and the reproduction of the systematic stratification of the black population during the transition from slavery to emancipation can be explained on four grounds. First, starting points were not the same across the whole black population. Those who were better off before emancipation – for example, the free persons of colour and the skilled slaves – had by and large a better chance to be upwardly mobile than the field or unskilled slaves. Second, emancipation abolished the system of slavery, but not the practice of discrimination. It took time to uproot old habits and conservative ways of life and thought. Third, the structure of opportunity was not the same for everyone. Access to jobs was not the same, nor was the ability to exploit contracts or to develop a good, practical understanding of the job market. Fourth, the hierarchy of environments and social services segregated the city along class lines. Every country – and for that matter every city – is made up of an hierarchy of environments. There are places that may provide more opportunities for upward mobility than others and where more social services are provided than elsewhere (Fontaine, 1986).

After emancipation a good number of freedmen who no longer wanted to work on their former masters' plantations fled to the cities, in some cases enlarging the existing slum settlements and in others creating new poor neighbourhoods (see also Goodenough 1978, p. 21). It was during this period that so-called 'Negro yards' and 'cours des miracles' were burgeoning in Kingston, Jamaica, and Fort-de-France, Martinique.[5]

In the second half of the nineteenth century, some East Indian, Chinese, and Javanese immigrants also became urban dwellers, either because they were employed by townfolk or because they came to the city after they had completed the terms of their indentures in rural areas.[6] The presence of Chinese merchants, shopkeepers, and pedlars in Havana, for example, was the result of that urban migration. Already in 1870, when Samuel Hazard visited the city, Chinese labourers were busy at work at La Honradez, a very well-known paper cigar manufacturer in nineteenth-century Havana.[7]

The study of the evolution of the area in the nineteenth century is of utmost importance to our understanding of contemporary urban poverty in the Caribbean, because that was the period during which the capitalist state developed its myriad internal variations. Emancipation did not simply mean freedom for the slaves, but also the transformation of the old system into a new social dynamic, that is, the passage of slave societies from a bi-racial (black/white) into a multi-racial and ethnic environment.

The arrival of new immigrants who provided cheap labour in the cities and on the estates deserted by the former slaves consolidated the emerging capitalist state. The urban upper class became in some instances tied to the lower class through ethnic middlemen. These stood between both groups and served as gear wheels in the overall functioning of the system because of their commercial acumen or powers of leadership. Some immigrants became structurally visible because they occupied a significant economic niche in the city. Chinese shopkeepers (grocery retail trade) in Port-of-Spain, Trinidad, for example, became middlemen within their neighbourhoods and were well integrated in the social life of that city (see Johnson, 1987, p. 85).

The 'village movement' after emancipation had an interesting role in the social reproduction of poverty. In addition to the church-sponsored villages of Jamaica there were in rural Guyana villages created by ex-slaves (Thomas, 1984 pp. 18–19). The lands on which villages were established were acquired either through communal purchase or individual proprietorships. The formation of these villages prevented a large crowd of poor people from migrating to the capital city.

An important fact about urban poverty in the nineteenth-century Caribbean is that it was not linked with or brought about by industrialisation, which was almost non-existent. The cities of the area were not involved in mass industrial production. The marxist notion of the 'reserve army of the unemployed' may not be useful to explain the phenomenon of urban poverty here in the second half of the nineteenth century.

Until the Second World War, in fact, the major cities of the Caribbean were, by and large, pre-industrial. Of course a few local industries existed but none large enough to gather in a significant number of employees. One thinks of the tobacco industry in Cuba, geared to the production and exportation of cigars, and the Barbancourt factory in Port-au-Prince for the exportation of Haitian rum (Hazard, 1871, p. 145; Corvington, 1975). These local ventures did not and could not serve by themselves as major attractions pulling the rural population to either city. Because of this low level of industrialisation, rural migration to the cities was slow and sporadic.

The situation of Port-of-Spain, Trinidad, was slightly different. A large number of immigrants from the other English-speaking islands came to settle there during the second half of the nineteenth century. Many came from Barbados: these brought skills and fluency in the English language, and a few were able to join the police force or to serve as nurses in the hospitals and asylums. Still other Barbadians worked as domestic servants. That inter-island migration was encouraged in part by the beginnings of industrialisation in Port-of-Spain. Indeed Brereton (1979, p. 24) notes that 'there was a certain amount of light manufacturing industry at the turn of the century: several rum distilleries; the well known Angostura Bitters factory owned by the Siegert family; two coconut oil and fibre factories; factories manufacturing ice, chocolate, matches, carriages, soap, leather goods, beer and stout, cigarettes and cigars; and various iron and brass foundries and machine shops'.

The reproduction of poverty in the transition from the pre-industrial to the industrial phase, as in period of emancipation, has several explanations. There was a need for cheap labour to maintain low wages. With industrialisation the city attracted migrant labourers in search of employment. Industrialisation by invitation, which was meant to strengthen the local economy and provide jobs for the unemployed, ended by deepening the dependence of the islands on the outside world. Industrialisation by invitation in the Caribbean, as elsewhere, has generally led to the exploitation of labour, the maintenance of a marginal sector to feed industry, and tax exemptions that enlarge the industry's margins of profit.

Not until after the Second World War, when the industrialisation of the major Caribbean cities really got under way, first, in Havana, Cuba and in San Juan, Puerto Rico, and later in Kingston, Jamaica, and Port-of-Spain, Trinidad, and in the period after the English-speaking island territories won their independence from England, did massive rural migration to the Caribbean capital cities, North America and Europe become a routine feature of Caribbean life. Until the Cuban revolution, urban poverty was localised in specific neighbourhoods of the Caribbean cities and its spatial boundaries were known. Jamaica, for example, had experienced a tremendous increase in the poor Rastafarian population of West Kingston in the decade just before the independence of the island in 1962.

A series of events have helped shape the movement of the poor rural population to the capital cities. Accustomed to work in Cuba during the sugar cane harvest, Haitian and Jamaican labourers were no longer able to do so with the advent of the Castro regime in 1958 (Laguerre, 1987, p. 120). Foreign labour was no longer needed after the American-owned businesses were nationalised and Cuba shifted from a capitalist to a socialist-oriented economy. Since the passage of the American Immigration Act of 1965 and the British Immigration Act of 1966, which somewhat restricted immigration to England from the islands, individuals from the anglophone islands have redirected their migration pattern to the United States. As independent nations each island can now have its own quota – it need not use the small fraction of the former one assigned to Britain by the United States. Since the end of the Second World War, some of the rural poor who migrated to the capital cities have done so with the intent of continuing their migration to Europe or North America.

Although rural poverty is by no means negligible, there has been a massive transfer of poverty from rural to urban centres over a relatively short span of time. This transfer is the more visible because the new urban poor have become, if not more politically organised, at least more vocal. In fact they have been made so by politicians eager to get their votes.

The migration of rural people to the city in search of employment and higher wages, and as one step in the larger, international migration, has become part of Caribbean daily life. That mass of incoming migrants has had to adapt to the structural features of the urban space. Since housing has been insufficient, migrants tend to settle in well-established slums or to rent apartments or rooms scattered throughout the inner-city districts; but once these traditional centres of the urban poor reach their maximum capacity, the poor must establish themselves, legally or illegally, elsewhere in the city, building their shacks with whatever materials they can find. Hence the expansion of inner-city slums and the development of squatter settlements or shantytowns in the margins of Caribbean cities.

The existence of so many poor people in the capitals of the Caribbean has transformed those cities into large slums with here and there pockets of the upper and middle classes. It is clear that their sizeable presence in relation to the rest of the urban population has already had a negative impact on urban services and facilities. The poor, having been exploited over and over again by the élite, now live in large numbers in the cities and share the facilities developed earlier to meet chiefly the needs of the urban middle and upper classes.

In addition to the degradation of the physical landscape in particular and of urban life in general, the urbanisation of Caribbean poverty has had at least two other long-term effects. First, urban criminal activities have increased tremendously across the spectrum from minor to violent.[8] Urban riots with a radical political content have now an infrastructure to sustain them. The army and the police – who in some cases would prefer to back the claims of the poor because they live among them – have become ever more resentful of the material property of the élite, which they are paid to protect. Second, the urban poor are developing an ever more acute awareness of their exploitation by the urban élite. There are signs that in Haiti and Santo Domingo they are used to form the broad base of leftist political organisations. Politicians have begun to pay more attention to the poor neighbourhoods in the city as they become increasingly aware that these are electoral constituencies to be reckoned with at both national and local political levels. The time may not be too far distant when some city governments, like that in Fort-de-France, will be dominated, because of the vast display of urban poverty, by left-wing politicians and strategists.

Poverty has become more and more a general feature of Caribbean capital cities: it is no longer geographically located exclusively in certain districts but can be seen everywhere, even in proximity to bourgeois residences. That is a fundamental characteristic of the contemporary Caribbean city. By focusing on one such city – Fort-de-France, the capital of Martinique – the present study hopes to explain the reproduction of urban poverty in the context of that island (see Figure 1.1: Map of Fort-de-France).

URBAN POVERTY AS A STRUCTURAL SYSTEM

Material poverty has always been with us since the beginning of human civilisation. Although the phenomenon is not new, the institutional and societal frameworks in which it is found at different historical epochs require different types of explanations. Since Karl Marx, social scientists have sought to alleviate the burden of the poor by writing about their conditions, in the hope that once the problem is identified and documented something can be done about it. The explanations are most often ideologically grounded because they presuppose the assumption of a particular kind of societal organisation. Consequently responses to the problem of poverty, a variety of creative urban policies, are also expected to lead to the proper functioning of a specific, desired type of society.

As students of Caribbean urban environments, the reality of poverty cannot escape our notice. To study urban poverty is one way to approach and understand the urban system and the urbanisation process.

Analyses of urban poverty tend to focus on the mode of capitalist accumulation, on domination by the élite, and social inequality, on a particular type of subculture that leads to the idea of an enclave, and on the idea of individual failure, including psychological factors that may inhibit the person from succeeding (Allen, 1970; Marx, 1936; Weber, 1966; Lewis, 1961). To express it in a larger stroke: poverty is seen as related to deficiencies that can be manifested at various levels. Gilbert (1970, p. 3) leans towards a view of poverty that is reflective of inadequacies at the institutional, cultural, and biological levels. Mono-causal explanations of poverty may not cover the total range of institutional situations.

The controversial debate between Pierre Joseph Proudhon and Karl Marx in the middle of the nineteenth century was a turning point in the 'history of explanations' concerning poverty. After Proudhon wrote 'The Philosophy of Poverty' in 1846, Karl Marx replied in 1847 with his ideologically oriented treatise, 'The Poverty of Philosophy'.

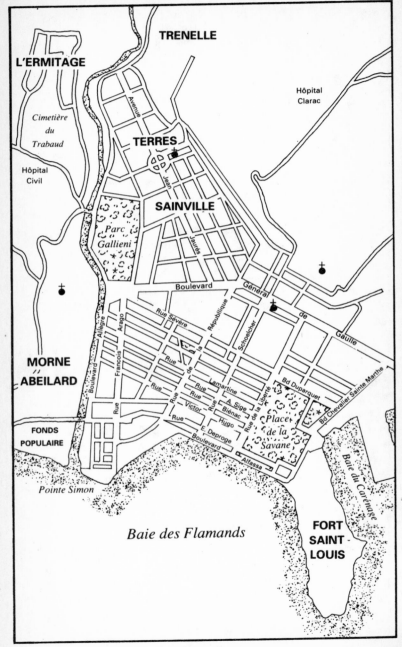

FIGURE 1.1   Detailed Map of Fort-de-France

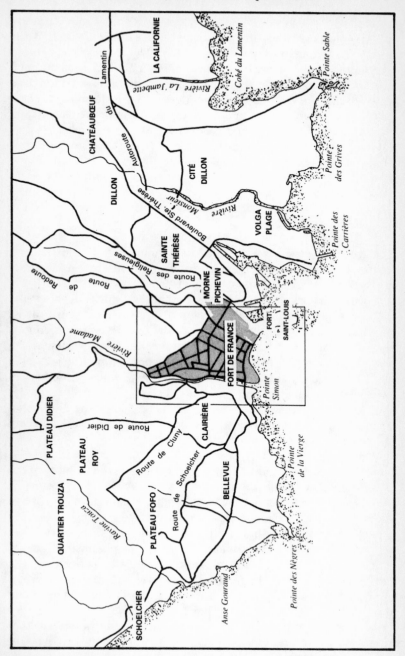

FIGURE 1.2 Fort-de-France and Surrounding Areas

Proudhon's study was an attempt at presenting a philosophical treatise on economical contradictions seen as a system. To accomplish that aim he indulged in an analysis of variables, such as value in use and value in exchange, the division of labour, machinery, competition, monopoly, police and taxation. In his reply Marx argued that it is not enough to philosophise about the issue: what matters is to transform the societal reality, or at the very least, to explain the problem in such a way that policies for change can be put forward and implemented. Marx's (1847, p. 174) ultimate revolutionary call is for the elimination of political power and the abolition of every class.

In the formulation of his law of capitalist accumulation Marx predicts that pauperisation of a segment of the labouring population is a *sine qua non* of the movement of modern industry. Indeed the author of *Das Kapital* (Marx, 1936, p. 707) writes:

> The greater the social wealth, the functioning capital, the extent and energy of its growth, and, therefore, also the absolute mass of the proletariat and the productiveness of its labour, the greater is the industrial reserve-army. The same causes which develop the expansive power of capital, develop also the labour-power at its disposal. The relative mass of the industrial reserve-army increases therefore with the potential energy of wealth. But the greater the reserve-army in proportion to the active labour-army, the greater is the mass of consolidated surplus-population, whose misery is in inverse ratio to its torment of labour. The more extensive, finally, the lazarus-layers of the working class, and the industrial reserve-army, the greater is official pauperism. This is the absolute general law of capitalist accumulation.

Studies in the marxist tradition continue to focus on the inability of the capitalist state to eradicate poverty in its midst. Poverty is seen as intrinsic to and manufactured by the capitalist system. In that light one may understand Wachtel's view on poverty. 'Examined from a perspective of radical political economics,' he states, 'poverty is the result of the normal functioning of the principal institutions of capitalism – specifically, labor markets, social class divisions and the state' (Wachtel, 1971, p. 1). In this straightforward marxist interpretation of human poverty, the villain, so to speak, is the capitalist state and its social apparatus.

Other social scientists prefer to focus on the cultural system that perpetuates or reproduces poverty. They propose three levels of explanation. At first we find the idea that the subculture provides all the negative mechanisms that hinder one's ability to escape the poverty cycle. This level assumes the notion of a subculture that maintains itself by socialising people into it. As Sarbin (1970, p. 31) puts it, 'The focus is less exclusively on the individual victims of poverty but rather on the social organization that creates specific social types that reproduce and maintain themselves with predictable regularity'. The second level of explanation leads us to the idea of individual failure. In this view of things a basic lack of motivation is the fundamental explanation to individual poverty. Achievement motivation, which is supposed to explain individual success, is defined 'in terms of concern for excellence in doing a task, as reflected in competition with the standards set by others or oneself; unique accomplishment; or long-term involvement in a task' (Pareek, 1970, p. 304; see also McClelland, 1961). That view tends to blame the victim for his shortcomings.

The third level expresses the idea that urban poverty is locational, that is, it can be localised in geographical space. It is produced in an enclave (Lewis, 1966). The culture of poverty needs an infrastructural basis of support and the peri-urban squatter settlement or inner-city slum provides such a niche.

A large majority of social scientists study poverty from a non-marxist structuralist perspective. In the Weberian tradition, poverty is seen as a by-product of social inequality. It is the result of structural shortcomings in the social system. For Weber poverty is an expression of social domination, a problem that can be solved through social reforms and a better integration of people in society (see Portes and Ferguson, 1975, p. 11). Moynihan and Banfield also see the problem as unavoidable in the context of American urbanisation, but at the same time realise that change within the system to ameliorate the life chances of the poor are possible. In a study of poverty in Mexico, Eckstein (1977a, p. 8) has argued that 'the life chances' of the urban poor . . . and their responses to their social and economic deprivation are largely by-products of societal class and power forces'.

Still other scientists focus, not on the causes of urban poverty, but rather on its positive functions. Gans (1972, p. 279) writes that 'the poor subsidize, directly or indirectly, many activities that benefit the affluent. For one thing, they have long supported both the consumption and investment activities of the private economy by virtue of the low wages they receive . . . . Poverty creates jobs for a number of occupations and professions which serve the poor . . . . The poor serve as symbolic constituencies and opponents for several political groups.'

In addition to looking at the state as producing poverty, some social scientists focus on the urban poor as strategists who seek for ways to overcome their burden. The literature on 'adaptive strategy' was developed as a reaction to the pathology that Oscar Lewis finds in the behaviour of the poor. Here the poor are seen not as ill but as choice-makers who may or may not succeed in their strategies. Often individual failure depends more on structural barriers than on presumed lack of motivation. Even with that positive twist, the literature on adaptive strategy presents an epistemological problem. One may refer to the lack of operationalisation of the concept of 'strategy'. It is an exaggeration to believe that the poor are always engaged in developing strategies. The poor man, like any other, is not always concerned about strategically managing his life. Such a view leaves no place for human freedom and the individual's ability to position himself at times outside the realm of economic rationality.

In this book I tend to explain poverty not simply in cultural terms – although I remain aware of cultural explanations – but rather in structural and situational terms. Spilerman and Elesh (1971, p. 362) note that 'cultural explanations of poverty argue that the behavior and attitudes of poor persons are components of a coherent lifestyle'. Whereas structural explanations focus on the inequality in the institutional make-up of the social system, situational explanations 'view the behavioral characteristics of low income individuals as an adaptation to environment and circumstances' (Spilerman and Elesh 1971, p. 362).

In this perspective poverty is seen as part of the process of capitalist accumulation. The capitalist behaviour that the poor may display willingly or unwillingly is not different from that of the bourgeois class. The poor are integrated in the process of capitalist accumulation through a series of intermediate institutions that provides the structural context for the maintenance of the system.

It may be said here that the poor, like the rich, participate in the process of accumulation. Though there is variation in wealth, there is also variation in poverty. There are individuals who are at the threshold of poverty, close to breaking through, and others at the bottom of the heap. There are those who have the skills to bridge the gap and others who do not have such skills. There are those who work hard so that the second generation can profit or benefit from their labour; there are others who do not think in those terms. There are those who used to be part of the middle class and for one reason or another – such as, for example, divorce – have become poor.

To understand the dynamics of this class of unfortunate people it is important to analyse its members in terms of three categories: (1) individuals who were born into poor families and have remained poor throughout their lifetimes, (2) the transitional poor, and (3) those who were not born in poverty but have become poor.

The size of the underclass does not depend solely on individual successes, but can also be influenced by structural weaknesses in the economy, by a lack of government interventions on behalf of the poor, and by the inability of the state to get to the root causes of poverty. When there is a lack of employment, that lower class is likely to expand; and in time of an employment boom it is likely to contract.

URBAN POVERTY AS A REPRODUCTIVE SYSTEM

To understand the operation of urban poverty one must also study the mechanisms of its reproduction. Reproduction may be the largest factor in understanding the functioning of the phenomenon.

The reproduction of poverty means the maintenance of power domination and the existence of a structure of inequality. Dialectically it implies the reproduction of the structure and the relations of domination, on the one hand, and the structure of dependence and inequality, on the other. Although in this book I posit the structure of domination as a given, my effort will be aimed at explaining poverty from below. This is simply a methodological strategy reflected in the content of data gathered for this study.

The concept of social reproduction has been used in the scholarly literature in three major ways: in the educational field to show how the school system reproduces the system of priveleges in society; in the 'culture of poverty' approach to argue that the subculture reproduces itself intergenerationally; and also in the marxist tradition as reproduction of power relations with or without Freudian connotations.

Bourdieu and Passeron (1970, pp. 225–37) are the two leading French theorists who advocate the view that the school is the main villain in the maintenance of the social order. For them the social function of the school system is that of reproduction of class relations. Students are socialised in such a way to replace those who are in key positions in society. The school helps to legitimise those positions and provides appropriate means to maintain the status quo. The values on which the society depends to survive are thoroughly taught. Students after graduation are normally ready to reproduce the system in order to reap the profit to which they believe they are entitled. A share in the system is considered their fair reward for so many years spent in school. In addition the school system selects and filters the future leaders of society through rules of admissions, rules of performances, rules of qualification, and rules of etiquettes. In other words the school legitimises the values that sustain power relations in society and produces the individuals to fill the positions that sustain those power positions.

Bourdieu (1971, p. 45) further distinguishes cultural reproduction from social reproduction. He argues that by contributing to the reproduction of the structure of distribution of the cultural capital among social classes, the educational system contributes immensely to the reproduction of the system of domination. It is also true that children of educated families have a better chance to succeed in life than those from poor families. As parents transmit their cultural capital to their children, the children are better equipped to understand the symbolic code of success in society. The investment of the parents in the schooling of their children is part of the overall 'system of strategies of reproduction' to ensure their well-being.

Yves Barel (1972, p. 61), however, brings more subtlety into the analysis of the concept of social reproduction. First and foremost, he sees reproduction as following the same laws as the process of production. For that matter he understands biological and social reproduction to be particular cases of the general phenomenon of reproduction. He notes that 'at the level of a determined system, biological reproduction is a process of duplication while social reproduction is a process of growth' (Barel, 1972, p. 113). Social reproduction is also seen as an individual and population phenomenon. He clarifies the idea that the reproduction of a subsystem is at the same time the reproduction of the metasystem and vice-versa. However, the reproduction of the subsystem and the reproduction of the metasystem are potentially contradictory. He further argues about 'the existence of a population of social systems hierarchically articulated. Social reproduction is at the same time the reproduction of those hierarchies and the reproduction of their constitutive elements' (Barel, 1972, p. 159).

According to theorists of the culture of poverty, poverty is reproduced because of the negative traits that such a subculture produces. The cultural environment is seen on the one hand as an hindrance to the individual's upward mobility and on the other hand as producing transgenerational poverty. As Spilerman and Elesh (1971, p. 369) note, 'The essential feature of a culture of poverty argument is that the value structure forms a self-maintaining system which perpetuates itself from generation to generation'.

In the marxist tradition reproduction implies both 'the reproduction of the means of production [and] the reproduction of the relations of production' (Lefebvre, 1976, p. 46). One may turn to Dickinson and Russell (1986, p. 1) for a brief summary and synthesis of the neo-marxist perspective on social reproduction. They note that 'broadly speaking, the social reproduction literature takes the dominant relationship of our time – the wage labour/capital relationship – as its principal object of analysis and considers the institutions, mechanisms and processes associated with the economic, social, political and ideological reproduction of the relationship. Of central importance here is the social construction of the factors of material production (land, labour and capital) and in particular, the social construction of human labour power as a commodity in capitalist society.'

The major focus of this book is on the mechanisms and institutions that shed light on the production of inequality and, in turn, explain the reproductive process of urban poverty. Basically the thrust will be to show that the reproduction of social relations has its own dynamic in which the larger structure of domination takes, so to speak, the actor's role in the process. Unlike Lewis I see the poor engaged in a struggle to escape poverty. It is evident that some succeed but that others do not. In the context of the capitalist state I understand the urban system as a flow of processes in which lies the possibility for one to change one's status for better or worse. The reader will be engaged here in the deconstruction of the micro-institutions that contribute in various ways to the manufacture and the reproduction of poverty.

In general other poverty theorists have placed the accent on the individual, the culture, or the state. My focus is on structural and situational contexts that breed, maintain and reproduce poverty, a focus that recognises the complementarity of individual, culture, and state. The book provides an analysis of the content, operation, and dynamics of these contexts, all of which are strategic to an understanding of the manufacture and the reproduction of urban poverty.

RESEARCH METHODS

To explain the process of the reproduction of urban poverty, I have
selected the island of Martinique and more specifically the capital city
of Fort-de-France. Martinique, colonised during the era of slavery by
the French, and for a short period by the British, was transformed into
a Department of France in 1946. Like all the capital cities of the
Caribbean, Fort-de-France has its share of poverty. Poverty here is not
simply geographically localised in the squatter settlements and inner
city slums, but can also be seen elsewhere throughout the city.

I spent the month of May, 1985, in Paris and Bordeaux reading and
analysing the extensive French literature – not available in the United
States – on Martinique. Before starting the actual field work in
Martinique, I had familiarised myself with the scholarly l..erature on
the island through various courses that I have been teaching on the
sociology of Caribbean societies.

Around mid-June of 1985, I left for Fort-de-France, having already
decided what specific issues I was going to investigate in connection
with my ongoing interest on urban poverty. I began my investigation in
two neighbourhoods – namely, Sainte Thérèse and Volga Plage. One
is an inner city slum and the other a squatter settlement.

I spent the summer interviewing approximately one hundred people
in each neighbourhood about yard life, family organisation, rotating
credit associations, immigrant problems, domestic servants, and the
functioning of grocery shops. In addition to these informants, I also
interviewed housekeepers and employers who were identified through
personal contacts I developed at the Agency for Urban Planning
(ADUAM). My research strategy in those neighbourhoods was to
select three streets or alleys and to interview the heads of the
household and other adult members in each house. The streets and
alleys were selected on the basis of issues studied.

Because two recent quantitative surveys undertaken by ADUAM
and the Bureau of Statistics (INSEE) were made available to me, my
concentration in the study was on qualitative data. Before I
interviewed the inhabitants of a house, I was familiar with the
quantitative data that were available in terms of sex, marital status,
income, education, religion, and weekly expenses of the household. I
was also able to retrieve this information from the census tracts, and as
my research proceeded, I verified the census information. Since the
census was taken just a few years before I began my research, I found
that most of the quantitative information the government gathered

was accurate. This situation had the effect of forcing me rather to concentrate on qualitative sociological data. Unlike so many previous studies on the Caribbean, mine does not begin with matrifocality, but rather on gathering information about the entire family as a multiproduct firm, and about other social aspects of family life as well.

Not all the information gathered during the research is presented here. I have selected the data that are of some importance in the formulation of my argument. I discussed the data again and again with the researchers at ADUAM. Their daily questions and comments forced me to return to the neighbourhoods to verify specific aspects of the research or get more information on some issues. Sometime ADUAM even pointed out some areas that I should investigate.

Not only was I able to consult on a regular basis with the other researchers at ADUAM, but I was also invited to present my preliminary findings in two public lectures to the Martinican academic community. These lectures provided the material for the lively discussion that ensued afterwards.

I returned to Martinique in February 1986 for more research. I had an opportunity during this stay to spend some time at the Centre de Recherches Caraïbes de l'Université de Montréal in Fonds Saint Jacques. I read there various master's theses and doctoral dissertations presented at the University of Montreal and in France on Martinican society, culture and history. I also discussed there the chapter on Saint Lucian, Dominican, and Haitian immigrants at an interdisciplinary symposium on inter-Caribbean migrations, sponsored and financed by the University of Montreal.

OVERVIEW OF THE CHAPTERS

The book develops the idea that poverty is reproduced through various local institutions and explains how such processes function. The first chapter presents the conceptual framework that will guide us through developing a perspective on urban poverty and social reproduction. Poverty is presented as a structural phenomenon with cultural implications. Its reproduction is seen also, in structural terms, as a result of a dialectical relationship between the dominant and exploited sectors of society.

The second chapter describes and compares two local niches where urban poverty survives: an inner-city slum and a squatter settlement. While the physical landscape of the squatter settlement has changed over the last twenty years, the inner-city slum has also made some progress. The different outcomes of these two settings are seen in terms of different strategies of intervention developed by the city government. In contrast to the inner-city slum the city government has been quick to help ameliorate the living conditions of that squatter settlement and integrate the residents into the larger society.

Chapter 3 focuses on a strategic institution, that is, the organisation of the urban family-household. Here the household is viewed as a multiproduct firm. This economic orientation does not pretend to shed light on the multifaceted nature of the family in urban Martinique, but rather presents a point of view in regard to its economic rationale. Here the focus is on the role played by the household in the reproduction of poverty.

The family is again studied from a different viewpoint, that of the domestic servant, in Chapter 4. Examining the role of the domestic servant helps to clarify the dependence of the lower class on the upper class. Most of the housekeepers work in those microniches that manufacture and reproduce poverty. Their participation in promoting the welfare of two households – their place of work and their own house – present us with an original way of studying family life and offers many insights into the world of the housekeeper.

Chapter 5 focuses on a strategic institution, the boutique or grocery shop. A series of economic transactions are done here on a daily basis. Although the boutique is located close to the lower-class people and meets their daily needs, it also serves in the neighbourhood as an agent of exploitation. Retail prices are by and large higher than for the same merchandise purchased in a supermarket. Since most of the businesses in Martinique are family owned and operated, a focus on small firms such as the boutique which provides a microsociological view on the relations between business and society in Martinique, is long overdue.

The economic life of the people is pretty much sustained by their participation in folk credit associations, such as the *Sousou*. This savings and credit association functions on a rotating basis, with each participating member receiving the fund in turn without any accruing interest. It will be found that not every member benefits economically from participation, the rewards being more social and psychological.

Chapter 7 investigates the conditions of poor immigrants from Saint Lucia, Haiti, and Dominica in Fort-de-France. The non-resident or illegal alien status of some of them is an impediment to upward mobility. English and Creole speaking migrants find themselves unable to compete with the lower-class Martinicans, who speak

French, understand the job market better, and in times of unemployment can fall back on their social security benefits. Both language and immigration status are formidable obstacles facing the newcomers. This chapter is a contribution to the growing body of literature on the sociology of inter-island migrations.

The concluding chapter places the Martinican case in the context of the Caribbean and synthesises some of the various urban policies developed for the region. It stresses the idea that urban poverty should be seen in the larger context of the economic development of the region, that Caribbean economies suffer from their dependent status, and that local governments need to develop and implement policies geared toward the elimination of urban poverty.

NOTES

1. Cuban historian Pedro Deschamps Chapeaux (1969) explains the causes of the escape of domestic slaves and documents the phenomenon of urban *marronage* in Havana.

2. Emilio Rodriguez Demorizi (1978), who wrote on urban life in Santo Domingo in the early sixteenth century, mentions the existence of the *Cofradia de la Concepcion de Nuestra Señora*. The members of this religious association provided logistic and financial support for the creation and maintenance of the Hospital of San Nicolas, the first modern hospital in the New World. He notes that 'las cofradias, congregaciones o hermandades de personas devotas reunidas para ejercitarse en obras de piedad y devocion cristiana, existieron en Santo Domingo desde los tiempos de Ovando – por el 1503' (Demorizi, 1978, p. 145).

3. Until 1791, spatial segregation was not enforced in Nassau and slaves lived in houses behind the residences of their masters. With the Haitian revolution (1791–1803), the urban black population was forced to settle outside the boundaries of the city (see Doran and Landis, 1980, p. 185).

4. Hall (1983, p. 17) speaks of 'a rapidly growing urban freedman population that increased, almost five-fold in the case of Christiansted and more than three-fold in the case of Fredericksted, between 1775 and the turn of the nineteenth century'. He further notes that 'in Charlotte Amalie as in Christiansted and Fredericksted, the urban slave population outnumbered whites and freedmen combined at the end of the eighteenth century' (Hall, 1983, p. 19).

5. The yards of Kingston, Jamaica, were studied by Brodber (1975) and the 'cours des miracles' of Fort-de-France, Martinique, by Pamphile (1985b). For Haiti, one must turn to Laguerre (1982) for a description

and analysis of urban yards in a depressed neighbourhood of Port-au-Prince.

6. On the East Indian, Chinese and Javanese immigration into the West Indies in the nineteenth century and their visible presence in the cities, see La Guerre (1974), Malefijt (1963) and Fried (1956).

7. See Hazard (1871). The Chinese population in Cuba was estimated to be more than 10 000 in 1911 (see Lindsay, 1911, p. 115).

8. Georgetown, Port-of-Spain, Santo Domingo, San Juan, Kingston, and Port-au-Prince are the Caribbean capital cities most affected by the rise of urban violent crimes. For example, the remarks made by De Albuquerque et al concerning Kingston could also be made about Port-au-Prince. They note that 'many areas of West Kingston are not passable at night, and the middle and the upper classes in the suburbs live in constant fear of being robbed or attacked. They are virtually subject populations by night, hiding behind high fences, steel bars, fierce dogs, and security guards. This fear has extended to all of Kingston's residents, and in many ways the urban poor are much more exposed to violent crime' (De Albuquerque et al, 1980, p. 382). For the evolution of criminal activities in Fort-de-France, Martinique, see particularly Demogeot and Roger (1976).

2 The Ecology of Urban Poverty

The slums and squatter settlements in the Caribbean are the breeding grounds for the reproduction of poverty, chiefly because of the concentration of urban dwellers to be found there. As one observes the total landscape of any primate Caribbean city, one begins to understand that there is often a correlation between poverty and space. There are several reasons for that. For example, the rural poor who migrate to the city, unless they have relatives in other parts of the town, tend to settle in the lower-class neighbourhoods. Further, because there is always speculation in land, the élite usually buy up what are perceived to be the best locations, and the most marginal land is left to the poor.

The social class to which one belongs influences the choice, or lack of choice, of the location in which one lives. Class status often leads to territorial segregation in the same way that race is a factor in the demarcation of residential areas in South Africa and the United States. It is of crucial importance to study the place where the poor live, so as to have a better understanding of the ecology of urban poverty.

Space is not a totally neutral entity or a pure concept. It can be a contributing factor in the reproduction of poverty. One can only agree with Lefebvre (1976. p. 83) when he notes that 'reproduction . . . is located not simply in society as a whole but in space as a whole . . . . The productive forces permit those who dispose of them to control space and even to produce it . . . . Space is distributed into peripheries which are hierarchised in relation to the centres; it is atomised . . . . Space as a whole has become the place where reproduction of the relations of production is located.'

To explain the ecological texture of urban poverty in Martinique, the organisational structure of two neighbourhoods will be examined: one is a very old inner-city slum – Lower Sainte Thérèse – whose origin as a slum dates back to the postemancipation period of the second half of the nineteenth century, and the other is a new squatter settlement that came into existence in the late 1950s. Although they have several features in common, they have followed somewhat different paths of development, in part because of different forms of intervention by the state. Pamphile (1985b, p. 76) explains the development of squatter settlements in Martinique as a response to demographic pressure following the Second World War. Unable to solve the housing problem, the city closed its eyes when the squatters began to occupy public land and to build shacks there. Volga Plage, Texaco, Pointe de la Vierge, Pointe de Jaham, have developed as a result of 'squatterisation' by incoming migrants.

FORT-DE-FRANCE

The city of Fort-de-France, formerly Fort Royal, begins its existence in 1637, during the administration of Du Parquet, when a fortress was built to house the military who would protect the rest of the colony.[1] It was however in the city of Saint Pierre, a very active commercial centre, that Du Parquet established the seat of his government. Later the administrations of Baas and Blenac slowly transformed Fort-de-France into the official administrative city of the colony. As early as 1671 a certain engineer, Payen, was hired to draw the limits of the city (Chauleau, 1966, p. 111). From that time on the colonists were allowed to build their houses, stores, and warehouses as long as they followed the plan of the city. However, as the site was very swampy, it was necessary to prepare the land further before the inhabitants could safely build their houses. The colonial government attended to the site preparations, and in 1695, when Father Jean Baptiste Labat visited the town, he found a few houses and a church owned by the Capuchins (Labat, 1724, II, p. 37). The major part of the town was owned by sugar plantation owners who, we are told, came to the city on Sunday to attend church services (Chauleau, 1966, p. 112).

The history of Fort-de-France during the colonial period is fundamentally the history, on the one hand, of social inequality between the colonists and their slaves and, on the other, of the control of the urban space by the European segment of society. Closed off from the status of whites, the space they occupied with their residences and their networks of influential contacts, the slaves were compelled to take their places at the bottom of colonial social order. During this period, space was already a factor as a locus of demarcation of social classes. The division of the colonial space followed class and sectoral interests as represented by the government employees (both military and civilian) who implemented the policies of the metropolitan crown, by the merchants who balanced their behaviour according to the law of supply and demand, and by the clergy who followed the directives from the overseas headquarters of the mission. Urban planning and policies were meant to integrate and articulate the local economy better with that of the French metropolitan centre.

During the period after emancipation in 1848, the physiognomy of the city did not change very suddenly. The former slaves were now freed, but Martinique remained a French possession and the white powerholders were still in a position to maintain control over the land and commerce. The freedmen congregated in the pre-existing and newly-developed urban yards, as they were called, and were mostly dependent on the local white population for employment. As the yards were unable to contain the poor black population, the black urban dwellers pushed beyond them and gradually transformed sections of the city into slums.

During the nineteenth century, the population of the city grew slowly: in 1853 there were 13 130 inhabitants; in 1876 there were 17 617. At about the same time, in 1850, the diocese of Fort-de-France was created and a bishop, Monsignor Le Herpeur, appointed to head it (see Joyau, 1967, p. 56). From 1862, when the *Compagnie Générale Transatlantique* started to provide services to the local population via its vessel *Louisiane*, the port of Fort-de-France became much more active. The *Louisiane* provided the main transportation for people and goods from Martinique to metropolitan France (Joyau, 1967, p. 57). The company was a source of jobs both for city dwellers and incoming migrants through the increase in port activities.

Hindered by hurricanes and fires, the city was slow to develop and expand physically. During the summer of 1887, the American writer Lafcadio Hearn visited Fort-de-France as a tourist, and provided us with one of the few descriptions of the city after the abolition of slavery in Martinique. 'Rebuilt in wood after the almost total destruction by an earthquake of its once picturesque streets of stone, Fort-de-France has little of outward interest by comparison with Saint Pierre. It lies in a low, moist plain, and has few remarkable buildings: you can walk all over the little town in about half an hour. But the Savane, – the great green public square, with its grand tamarinds and sabliers, – would be worth the visit alone, even were it not made romantic by the marble memory of Josephine' (Hearn, 1923, p. 58).

Probably one of the most important events of the turn of the century was the arrival in Fort-de-France on 30 March 1894, of the King of Dahomey, Boiadjere Bowele Behanzin. He was deposed and exiled to Martinique by the French government. One of his sons attended the school run by the Brothers of Ploermel in Fort-de-France and later the Lycée of Saint Pierre (Joyau, 1967, p. 57).

Although Fort-de-France had been the seat of the government for many years, Saint Pierre remained a significant rival because of its large Béké (descendants of French colonists) population. This situation changed abruptly in 1902 with the volcanic eruption of Mount Pelée. That eruption had a number of consequences for the city of Fort-de-France. Marieu (1977, p. 1) has estimated that 'about three fourths of the Béké population had died during the volcanic eruption at Mount Pelée in 1902'. In the years following that eruption, Saint Pierre was no longer an important competitor. There had been a great loss of life in that city and many buildings destroyed. Fort-de-France became overnight not only the administrative but also the commercial, trading, and shipping centre of the island. It got a share of the Béké population from Saint Pierre, who started rebuilding their villas in the Didier neighbourhood of the city, and its port became more active and vigorous than ever. In 1902 the population of Fort-de-France was 24 692 inhabitants; by 1931 it had doubled in size and numbered 48 395 inhabitants.

The city gathered into its midst not only the upper-class Béké population but also poor migrants. The Terres Sainville neighbourhood began to expand. The Terres Sainville was in the beginning a plantation, and was later sold to the private *Société des Faubourgs Thébaudière*. This company subdivided the land, and sold and rented some portions to poor people who built their shacks on the property. In 1925 the city council acquired the land and began to develop the area as an integral part of the city. This former '*quartier misérable*' was now provided with paved streets, electricity, water fountains, and a church, and some old-timers were able to return to their renovated neighbourhood (Sévère, 1931, p. 281). The poorest residents, however, left and never returned; instead they established themselves in Sainte Thérèse, known also as the Terres Porry, for the person who used to own that piece of land (Revert, 1949, p. 303).

The social atmosphere of the Terres Sainville is recounted by one of its inhabitants. Labetan (1982, p. 7) remembers the peripatetic breadfruit vendors who crisscrossed the streets of the neighbourhood in search of buyers. These individuals were not residents of Terres Sainville but rather came from surrounding neighbourhoods and hills, such as Ermitage, the Trénelle Zone and the Cour Fruit-à-Pain.

After informing us that the school in Terres Sainville was built in 1929 as the replacement of the older Rochambeau Institution, and that the neighbourhood is known for its *quarante-deux marches* (forty-two steps) leading to a hilly section of the town, Labetan describes the biggest house in Terres Sainville, known as La Maison Perron and located on Brithmer Street. He notes that 'with its two floors and covering an area of about sixty-four square meters, it was the most important house in Terres Sainville. The first floor served as a retail shop and a storage of rum. An official of the French government lived on the second floor' (Labetan, 1982, p. 9).

The period after the Second World War saw an acceleration in the growth of the city. Elizabeth (1977, p. 3) estimates that whereas in 1954 one-third of the population lived in the cities, by 1967 it was completely the reverse, with only one-third living in the rural areas. He argues that the city of Fort-de-France alone accounts for more than half of the growth of the national population. The influx had as an immediate effect the restructuring of power relations in the city's political, economic and social arenas. Population pressures were also a critical factor in the shaping of the city's landscape. From 1954 to 1967, the population of Fort-de-France increased from 60 648 inhabitants to 96 943. Letchimy (1985, p. 126) remarks that 'this massive urbanization, because it was not accompanied by an equal effort of planning, housing construction, and economic development has caused very rapidly serious problems of organization and control of the urban space'. Pamphile (1985b, p. 74) further argues that unplanned urban development in Martinique is the result of two factors. On the one hand, squatters invade public land without being evicted by the national or city government, and on the other, individuals build additional houses on their property without state intervention and knowledge.

The enlargement of Fort-de-France both in physical area and in population came about as a result of structural changes in the local economy. It represents a shift away from the plantation economy and the growth of the industrial sector. The multiplicity of social services and jobs in the new economic sector, and welfare provided to the unemployed and the handicapped are a few of the factors that have contributed to make Fort-de-France a magnetic pole attracting the rural population (see Letchimy 1985, p. 126).

By 1967 Fort-de-France had already become a primate city. Marieu (1977, p. 6) estimates that 'in 1967, 40 per cent of its inhabitants were born outside of the city limits'. This tells us much about the increase rate in the rural-urban migration movement on the island. The primacy in 1967 of Fort-de-France can also be illustrated in terms of the concentration of jobs and services. Genteuil (1977, p. 1) notes that 'in 1967 61 per cent of state employees, 63 per cent of employees in the private sector and 78 per cent of individuals in the liberal professions live in Fort-de-France'. In a survey of 232 migrants, all of them former residents of the village where he carried out his research, Levy (1976, p. 109) has found that 42 per cent resettled in Fort-de-France, 38 per cent in metropolitan France, 13 per cent in other Martinican villages and 7 per cent in North America and other French territories.

The shape of the urban space is still very much influenced by the business district, which in Fort-de-France is characterised by a number of small stores owned and operated by whites, Syrio-Lebanese and light-skinned Martinicans. The Syrio-Lebanese presence in Martinique, as in the other islands, is considerable. Réaud (1977, p. 1) observes that 107 out of 299 clothing, textile, and shoe shops found in Fort-de-France belong to Syrio-Lebanese merchants. They virtually control the commerce in the François Arago Street, where they own twenty-three of the twenty-nine clothing and shoe shops.

The major public market of Fort-de-France, located at the centre of the city, is bounded by Antoine Siger Street, Blenac Street, and Isambert Street. It is divided into a large central market-place on the one hand, where one can buy fruits and vegetables, and the annexe, or the little market, on the other hand, where one can buy meat. Neighbouring streets on certain days are transformed into what Martinican urban geographer Glondu (1983, p. 12) called 'spontaneous markets'. Two other markets, Gallieni and Lafcadiohearn, located in the margins of the business district, help to ease the congestion of the main market.[2]

The city of Fort-de-France is sandwiched between two bedroom communities, Schoelcher and Lamentin. The latter is of some importance in the life of the city since it is home of the international airport and a good number of industries (see Genteuil 1977, p. 1). Centre of national social life, port city, headquarters of both the mayoral and prefectoral administrations, bridgehead between Martinique and metropolitan France and connecting link with the other French territories, Fort-de-France in addition provides many niches for the large population of poor urban dwellers. Sainte Thérèse and Volga Plage are only two examples of such niches of poverty within the geographical boundaries of the city.

VOLGA PLAGE: THE DEVELOPMENT OF A SQUATTER SETTLEMENT

Speaking geographically, a squatter settlement arises from the illegal occupancy of public or private land and the development of a makeshift neighbourhood in the physical margins of the city by incoming lower-class migrants. Speaking economically, a squatter settlement indicates the existence of a reserve-army of the unemployed, the role of which is to provide both services and a clientele to the local urban market economy, and which is of utmost importance in the functioning of the informal sector of the economy. Speaking politically, it means a source of votes to the politicians and, if organised, an interest group capable of pressuring the city council on issues pertaining to the well-being of the neighbourhood. Speaking epidemiologically, it is a breeding ground for all kinds of diseases and a potential health hazard for the rest of the urban community.

The squatter settlement of Volga Plage came into existence after the Second World War, more precisely in 1959, as part of the massive migration of the rural population to the island's primate city. Known previously as 'Valmeunière', Volga Plage has an area of approximately thirteen hectares and is located in the eastern side of Fort-de-France and on the left side of Rivière Monsieur (Humbert, 1975, p. 3).

Even before the invasion of the squatters, the district was not totally devoid of inhabitants. A few shacks belonging to fishermen had already sprung up there. These were scattered and did not attract the attention of the city, since the area was a bit swampy within the limits of the *'cinquante pas géométriques'*[3] and the fishing population minded its own business. In the beginning, therefore, the area was not considered a problem for the city.

The creation of Volga Plage as a squatter settlement would probably never have occurred if it were not for a policy conflict between the offices of the mayor and the prefect. On 22 September 1958, the mayor requested that the city be given permission to transform the area into a recreational facility with public baths, a botanical garden, and installations for camping and yachting (Humbert, 1975, p. 3). The prefecture did not acquiesce to the mayor's demand, and by 1961 the squatters had the place well under control. When the government decided to expel the squatters by military might, the mayor objected. His office was in no position to provide squatters with decent housing once they had been evicted, and furthermore he saw in them potential voters who would contribute to the growth and success of his party.

Humbert (1975, p. 4) has delineated the sequence followed by the squatters who settled in the area. Typically they started by delimiting the area in which they wanted to settle with a rough sort of fence, enclosing from 100 to 800 square metres depending on the aggressiveness of the squatter. While they still lived in the community of origin, they assembled and prepared the wood for the construction of a house. When this material had been transported to Volga Plage by sea or by land, slowly the house was erected, with the help of family members and friends, most of the work being done on weekends. The house was frequently occupied before it was completed.

Once settled, squatters might engage in buying and selling. Portions of the area under the control of one squatter might be sold to friends and relatives. These transactions brought in some cash and also encouraged family members and former neighbours to settle together. Gradually the squatters would rely more on this newly-settled area than on the previous residence, and invested more on the new house, as shown in a transformation from wood frame to cement blocks, and in enlargements and embellishments. At this time the structure became the family's principal house.

The city began to intervene in a systematic fashion in the 1970s when Volga Plage became a problem for the rest of the population. The area was provided with minimal facilities and services, such as running water, electricity, and garbage collection, as a way of keeping the inhabitants quiet and integrating the neighbourhood into the structure of the city.

By 1975 the integration of Volga Plage had been achieved. Where in 1960 there had been seventy-seven wood frame houses in Volga Plage, by 1962 there were 586. Because some of those were transformed into cement block houses, only 413 wood houses remained in Volga Plage by 1975. In 1960 there had been no cement block houses, but by 1962 there were sixteen that had a single floor and one with two floors. By 1975 there were 393 with one and 144 with two floors. In June of 1975 sixty-five additional cement block houses were under construction (Humbert, 1975, p. 5).

A survey of twenty-nine Volga Plage households found 20.69 per cent consisted of single persons, 48.27 per cent of husbands, wives and children; 27.59 per cent were women heads of household with children; 3.44 per cent were headed by men with children. Among the women who were heads of households, approximately one-third were divorcees or widows.

Volga Plage now forms a stable population. The results of the survey indicate that the majority of its residents (57.07 per cent) are no longer rural migrants, but were born in Volga Plage or in other neighbourhoods of the city. The remaining inhabitants are migrants from other villages (40.78 per cent) and foreign-born from Dominica, Panama and Saint Lucia (6.15 per cent) (see Table 2.1)

TABLE 2.1   *Birthplaces of Volga Plage Residents*

	%
Martinique	
Anse D'Arlet	1.54
Bassepointe	3.85
Ducos	0.77
François	2.31
Gros Morne	2.31
Lamentin	5.38
Macouba	1.54
Marigot	1.54
Marin	2.31
Rivière Pilote	0.77
Rivière Salée	0.77
Robert	1.54
Sainte Marie	4.61
Saint Esprit	1.54
Schoelcher	2.31
Trinité	3.85
Trois Islets	2.31
Vauclin	1.54
Volga Plage (Fort-de-France)	53.07
Dominica	3.07
Panama	0.77
St Lucia	2.31
N = 130 (29 households)	

SAINTE THÉRÈSE: THE DEVELOPMENT OF AN INNER-CITY SLUM

Whereas the squatter settlement begins as an invasion of the land by incoming migrants, the slum develops over a lengthier period. It is a product of a history of dependent relationships between the poor and the local bourgeoisie. The mechanisms explaining its existence, however, do not differ qualitatively from those of the squatter settlement. Poor people attracted to the city for employment find themselves at the bottom of the social structure. The exploitation of the slum dwellers has been constant over time. The history of Sainte Thérèse attests to the structural marginality of the neighbourhood in the Fort-de-France metropolitan area.

Sainte Thérèse is divided into two distinct and recognisable zones. Upper Sainte Thérèse is situated for the most part in low hills and the vast majority of its residents are middle class. It thus stands clearly in contrast with Lower Sainte Thérèse, which is a poor neighbourhood. Genteuil (1977, p. 2) notes that 'the parish of Sainte Thérèse, with its 10,714 inhabitants, dominates the port of Fort-de-France and constitutes a popular and active neighbourhood. Until the construction of the first portion of the route de Rocade of Fort-de-France, the Boulevard Sainte Thérèse was the only road that linked the capital city to most parts of the island. This neighbourhood developed around this principal boulevard and the church located on the top of the Morne Pichevin. The wooden houses were for the most part built on the side of the Morne, which has an altitude of thirty metres.'

Lower Sainte Thérèse, the area bounded by Boulevard Maurice Bishop, Canal Alaric, Ravine Moreau and the Route de la Baie des Tourelles, is the oldest inner-city slum in Fort-de-France. It began as a peri-urban slum. The transformation of Fort-de-France into the capital city of the island after the volcanic eruption at Mount Pelée in 1902, the creation of a parish containing Upper and Lower Sainte Thérèse, and the ecological change resulting from new construction by lower-class in-migrants, gradually turned Lower Sainte Thérèse into an inner-city slum. The first inhabitants of Sainte Thérèse were dockers associated with the port of Fort-de-France, surplus population evicted from Terres Sainville when the city acquired that land in 1925, and rural migrants in search of employment.

The population of Sainte Thérèse began to grow substantially more dense in the thirties. It is worth quoting Joseph Zobel (1980, p. 126), the Martinican novelist whose book *La Rue Cases Nègres* was made into the movie *Sugar Cane Alley*. As a young boy in the thirties he came to live with his mother in Sainte Thérèse, and his memories offer a valuable description of the landscape:

A sizable black population of workers – the overflow from the other slum-filled, malaria- and typhoid fever-infested districts of the town – flocked to the area and, on both the initiative of each person and epic zeal, set up a huge encampment. Five or six alleys had been traced out, paved in any old fashion, and given names whose origin or meaning no one knew. Along those alleys, there sprang up a line of the standard type of shacks: huge boxes that had contained imported American cars, set gingerly on concrete or dried stones or on mere wooden stilts, and covered with eight sheets of galvanized aluminum. Often the roof consisted of a multitude of more or less rusty tins, smashed in, out, flattened and laid out like scales of a fish.

Not every newcomer was able to build his or her own shack. Some individuals took advantage of this disparity of means to build dwellings to rent to those who could not afford to own. Often these landlords had homes already somewhere in the city for their families and were able to make some extra income by providing housing to the neediest. Zobel (1980, p. 127) informs us that his mother was in the latter category and was forced to rent from a local landlord.

The transformation of Lower Sainte Thérèse into an inner-city slum was encouraged by its proximity to the harbour of Fort-de-France. The first buildings in the area were stores and warehouses belonging to Békés engaged in the import/export sector of the economy. Adjacent to these were smaller dwellings to accommodate the watchmen and their families as well as the dockers who loaded, unloaded and repaired the ships. The workers were allowed to live here because, in the first place, low-income housing was unavailable in the city proper; then, it was possible to use unoccupied state land, the '*cinquante pas géométriques du Roi*' (state land left uninhabited for protection of the local population in case of foreign invasion and for military exercise).

Ever since Martinique became a Department of France in 1946, the area has been increasingly overpopulated, first by the dockers' extended families and also by the invasion of the area by rural migrants and immigrants from Saint Lucia, Dominica, and Haiti.[4] Behind the main boulevard, where the stores are located, are alleys or yards where people live and interact with each other daily.

One of the important factors in the social organisation of the Lower Sainte Thérèse slum is the 'yards', which are still in some cases family groups or compounds. Actually the entire area is made up of contiguous yards. Once we recognise the existence of these units, it is easier to understand the organisation of the urban space. The yard in its inception was a family economic unit with its own physical boundaries. It was owned by a proprietor who might or might not live there. The development of the yard as a conglomerate of houses depended largely on decisions made by the proprietor to rent or to sell some of his property to others. The physical shape of the yard does not remain the same over time. New constructions, emigration of residents, and immigration of newcomers are all part of the dynamic of the yard. To give a sense of the evolution and function of the neighbourhood, two of these yards will be studied, namely, Mangatale and Valère.

MANGATALE YARD

Mangatale Yard is located within the limits of the *cinquante pas géométriques*. According to my main informant, who happens to be a well-informed dweller in the area, a Béké plantation owner had built a warehouse there, probably with the permission of the city. It was soon transformed into a residence for his mistress, a woman named Mangatale. Like most persons named Mangatale living on the island, she was a coolie, a descendant of the East Indian immigrants who were recruited after emancipation from slavery in 1848 to work the sugar cane plantations. Although she died long before I began this research, the place is still known as Cour Mangatale. All the yards in Lower Sainte Thérèse are identified by the name of the owner-resident who first developed the place as a yard.[5] These names eventually are applied to administrative units since people use them to refer to those who live in those yards. Thus they serve also as post office addresses: to send a letter to someone who lives in a yard, one has to include the name of the yard in the address.

Around 1930 there were four houses on the property, the main house in which Mrs Mangatale and her two children lived, and three other houses that were rented out to the aunt and parents of the informant. Mrs Mangatale also rented a room in the main house to the parents of my informant. The last house was rented to a couple which was not related by blood to the other members of the yard.

In the beginning, with a small group of relatives living together in the yard, there was social cohesion, co-operation, and mutual aid in time of need. Through the institution of ritual kinship, links between households became stronger; Mangatale's daughter, for example, was the godmother of the informant's sister.

When the informant's mother came to the yard, she had four children – two daughters, Marie and Josée, and two sons. Three children had the same father. The children were, respectively, eleven, sixteen, eighteen, and twenty years old when they arrived together from Sainte Anne, a small town in the south of Martinique. Since the family could not afford to send the children to school, they all began working for a living as soon as they arrived in the city. The two daughters worked as domestic servants outside the yard. The eldest, Marie, had a child, Francine, when she was twenty-two years old; and later she married but did not have any children by her husband. Her daughter, Francine, another informant, is now fifty years old, a teacher in the public schools. She spends a good deal of time visiting with her mother, but she does not live in the yard. The other sister,

Josée, married and had four children. Both sisters are now enjoying the blessings of old age in the yard. The two sons became dockers and moved into apartments outside the yard. One of them has died; the other is a barman in Sainte Thérèse.

Until 1946 those houses were the only structures on the property. In the back of the yard there were coconut trees, and people grew maize, rice, and vegetables for their own consumption. At that time the yard was both a residence and a field for cultivation.

After departmentalisation other migrants from Sainte Anne became squatters on the land. Their arrival made renters aware of the possibility of their taking advantage of the state land as well. Since they were already occupying the ground, they started building their own shacks and returned the dwellings they were renting to Mangatale. As the old-timers put up their own houses, they were in a position to rent either whole dwellings or rooms to newcomers, which they did, thereby accumulating some cash.

In the early 1960s even more people came as squatters, but were forced to take the land near the canal, a humid mangrove terrain that is the worst land in the neighbourhood. Unwilling or unable to rent, the newcomers built their shacks as an appendix to the existing settlement. By the late seventies, the canal section was completely settled.

The Mangatale yard is made up of households, so it is important to give a brief account of their composition and history. A few of them are selected here for review (see Figure 2.1: Mangatale Yard).

House No. 1.   The occupant of this house is the son of a couple who live in another house in the yard. He does not pay any rent since the house belongs to his parents. By profession, he is a taxi driver.

House No. 2.   The occupants are a couple who own this house, built on state land. They came to the yard in 1983. Five children live with them, of which two are children of both the husband and the wife and three others are the wife's children by another man.

House No. 3.   A couple occupy this house rent free because the house is owned by the wife's mother. They are in their thirties and have two children.

House No. 4.   Owner also of House No. 3, this resident lives by herself. She acquired these properties in 1966 and now is enjoying her retirement years.

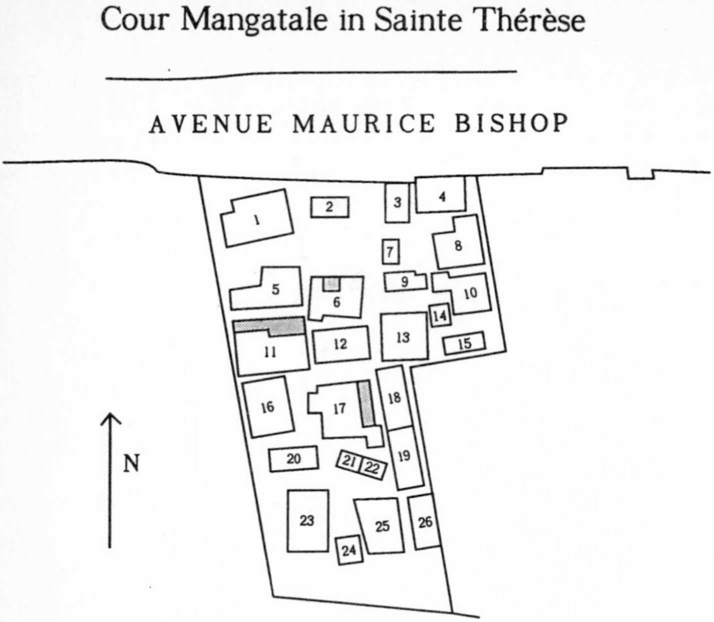
Cour Mangatale in Sainte Thérèse
AVENUE MAURICE BISHOP
N
1
2
3
4
5
6
7
8
9
10
11
12
13
14
15
16
17
18
19
20
21
22
23
24
25
26

FIGURE 2.1 Mangatale Yard.

House No. 5. This place is rented by a couple who came to the neighbourhood in 1963. They had three children.

House No. 6. The husband of this couple came to the yard in 1956 and the wife in 1974. They own the property and have six children.

House No. 7. This couple came to the neighbourhood in 1975. They rent their place from a neighbour. They have four children.

Houses No. 8 and No. 9. were vacant.

House No. 10. In this house live a retired couple. They came to the yard in 1971 and now own their house.

House No. 11. The couple who owns this house came to the yard in 1953. In addition to their three children, five grandchildren live with them.

VALÈRE YARD

This piece of property in proximity to the Mangatale Yard was part of a larger domain owned at the beginning of the nineteenth century by one Simbert Arthur. The land was later sold to Achille Himmer. However, the first official document attesting to transactions of this land dated of

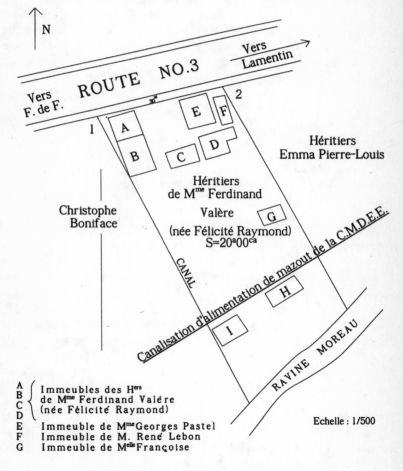

Cour Valère in Sainte Thérèse   Nov. 1948

FIGURE 2.2   Valère Yard in 1948.

26 May 1879, when Jules Sabas, a fisherman, and Marie Rose Camatchy, the daughter of a coolie store owner in Fort-de-France named Latchy purchased the property from Himmer. One year later, on 29 July 1880, they sold a portion of the property to Melle Félicité Raymond. Only one house existed on the property at that time. The new owner married Ferdinand Valère while living on her property, and the name Valère Yard comes from her husband.

On 15 November 1948, after the death of Mrs Valère, the property was registered with the Records Office (see Figure 2.2: Valère Yard in 1948). There were already nine houses on it, four of them belonging to the Valère children and five to individuals who had purchased pieces of the original property from the Valères. Figures 2.2 and 2.3 show the number of houses on the property in 1948 and 1985. The yard is made up of households and it is useful to document the kinship links that exist among the residents (see Figure 2.3: Valère Yard in 1985).

House No. 1.   This house belongs to Raymond Valère, who does not live there, but rents it to three people who occupy various rooms of the house. One is a photographer who rents a room on the first floor, which also serves as a photo shop where he conducts his business. The second renter also uses his room as a shop where he sells mechanical parts. The third renter, a woman, lives on the second floor with three children by two different fathers.

House No. 2.   This house belongs to Pierre Valère, the brother of Raymond. He built the house himself and lived in it while he was building it. He died shortly after it was finished, and the house was inherited by a woman friend who lived there and had two children by him.

House No. 3.   This house belongs to one Mr Bledin. There was no one living there when this research was conducted.

Houses No. 4 and No. 5.   These two houses belong, respectively, to the Anglio Melieu and Marcel Melieu families.

House No. 6.   This house used to belong to a Chinese man who purchased it earlier from the Valères, and used it as a grocery shop. It has been sold to another person who runs the shop.

House No. 7.   This house is occupied by immigrants from Saint Lucia. The woman who rents it has one child. The father, a Martinican, does

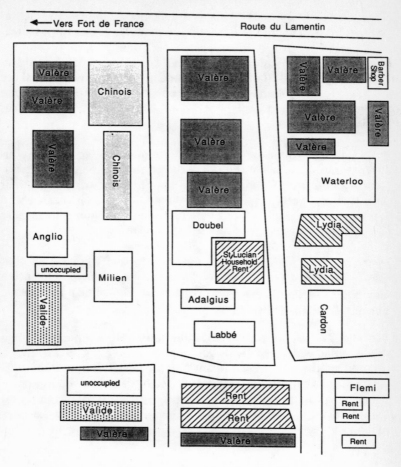

FIGURE 2.3 Valère Yard in 1985.

not live there. Her younger brother, who holds a British passport, is also living with her. She is engaged in trading, buying merchandise in Saint Lucia and reselling it in Fort-de-France.

House No. 8. This house belonged to Raymond Valère, the uncle of the Valère of House No. 1. The uncle is deceased and the boy who inherited the property lives in Paris. He rents the front room to a tenant who has turned it into a retail shop. The other rooms are empty and are a haven for marijuana smokers. Raymond Valère was known to be a *séancier* (magical specialist), and the people believe that he was successful in life because of his ability to manoeuvre the spirit world.

House No. 9.   This house is owned by the brother of the proprietors of Houses No. 8. and No. 10. The husband died and the wife lives there with four of her children and a niece. The father of one of the children lives in the same yard, in House No. 4. This child had had serious psychiatric problems.

House No. 10.   The sister of the proprietor of House No. 9 owned this house. Her husband was a veteran of the French campaign in Algeria. When the mother died, the children took the father to court to get their share of the property. The house is inhabited by the oldest son, who also has a young daughter living with him. That daughter is taken care of by an aunt who lives in another house in the yard.

House No. 11.   This house belongs to someone who has another house in the yard. It is rented to a Saint Lucian couple of which, the husband, at the time of this study, was in jail for killing a Martinican man during a quarrel in a bar.

House No. 12.   A docker occupies this house. He is reported to be a sexual maniac who sleeps with young girls while he is having affairs with their mothers. Since he financially supported the mothers, this has never been reported to the police. He has also the reputation of beating his girlfriends. He was once taken to a psychiatric hospital after he had killed somebody in the neighbourhood, but he lives quietly by himself.

House No. 13.   This house is also owned by a docker. He lives alone and is known to be a bit strange.

House No. 14.   This shack was built by a squatter, who has never been challenged by anyone to leave the place.

House No. 15.   This house belongs to a coolie couple. They have been living here since the late 1940s and have seven children. The husband is now paralysed.

Houses No. 16 and 17.   Both houses once belonged to a Seventh Day Adventist who was a good friend of the Valères. She had a small boutique (grocery shop) in one of the houses that catered to clients in the yard. After she died the two houses were rented to Haitian immigrants, who, according to neighbours, do not mingle with the other residents of the yard.

House No. 18.　This house was owned by a Valère, the sister of the owners of Houses No. 12, No. 19 and No. 22. However, she left for Guyana and lives there. A man named Waterloo, who rented the place for thirty years, finally bought it from her.

House No. 19.　The owner, Dolores, is a sister of the proprietor of House No. 1. She was married twice and now lives outside of the yard with a policeman. She takes care of the children of her unmarried brothers. The house is now rented to two nieces, of whom one is childless and the other has three children.

House No. 20.　The house is owned by Lucien Valère, the son of Raymond Valère. He used it for a while to store paints owned by a metropolitan French businessman. He moved to Paris after finding a better position there. The house was empty during the summer of 1985.

House No. 21.　This was a garage transformed into a house. It belongs to Pierre Valère.

House No. 22.　This house is rented and belongs to a Valère who now lives in Paris. She keeps a room in that house for the use of her son. The son, however, lives elsewhere in town.

House No. 31.　This house belongs to another son of Raymond Valère.

House No. 36.　This house belongs to a brother of Raymond Valère, who lives alone in the house. He is considered the shame of the Valère family because he is mentally handicapped.

THE URBAN YARD

During the course of my research in Martinique, I became aware of the importance of the yard in the spatial texture of the city. Later, as I started familiarising myself with the literature on urban yards in Kingston and Fort-de-France by Brodber and Pamphile, I was convinced that further investigations on the integration of yards within urban slums was greatly needed. The yards offer a route to understanding the atomisation of urban space and to engaging in deconstruction of its meaning.

Pamphile (1985a, p. 6) dates the origin of the urban yard to the beginning of the nineteenth century. As the colony was going through a major agricultural crisis, the local peasantry migrated to provincial towns in search of employment. Some slaves ('esclaves à billet') trusted by their masters were also allowed to migrate to the towns. This urban proletariat, which in some towns consisted mostly of slaves, became more important after abolition of slavery. A second migration, this time of freedmen, enlarged the existing urban proletariat.

These early yards were made to accommodate two groups of people: slaves and freedmen. They were developed by individuals who owned houses in the city with the idea of renting them to the incoming migrant population.[6] Conditions were far from hygienic in these disease-breeding environments, and a certain level of promiscuity prevailed (Pamphile 1985b, p. 75).

Pamphile (1985a, p. 6) provides us with a general description of the classic urban yard that prevailed early in this century in Fort-de-France, which encompassed both a space where the people lived and socialised among themselves and a garden area. He notes that 'generally speaking, the urban yard had a square or rectangular form. The rooms on the one side faced the ones on the other side and each one had an entrance door and a window. The common space, the alley, was the place where the people cooked their meals; it was also the ground used for community life. A good fountain provided fresh water to the residents. At the end of the alley, . . . there was a yard fifteen metres deep with several fruit trees'. Urban yards in Fort-de-France have a long history. Among the best known are la Cour Fruit à Pain, la Cour Clindor, la Cour Constantin, la Cour Marie Nelly, la Cour Valère, la Cour Mangatale and la Cour Cotrel.[7]

The yards in the business district of Fort-de-France have been for the most part destroyed. Constantin Yard, for example, which used to be located on Republic Street, no longer exists. This yard was made up, according to a member of the family who owned it, of two long houses facing each other and separated by an alley that served as the ground for social life and interaction among the residents (Pamphile 1985a, p. 6).

The yard fulfils a series of needs and functions in the slum of Sainte Thérèse. On the one hand, it provides cheap housing to the incoming poor migrant, who may not have any relatives in the city. On the other hand, it allows the local landlord to make money by renting extra rooms or apartments. As a source of temporary housing, it also contributes a solution to the housing crisis and, indirectly, to the maintenance of a certain climate of peace in the city.

The yards of Sainte Thérèse are still a focus of family interaction, although they comprise, in addition to sets of family residences, unrelated individuals and immigrants from other islands. Many persons make their first contact with city life through their socialisation in the yards. There are also several houses owned by individuals who have family in the yard but who themselves no longer live there. The people in the yard form a small universe through the sum of their daily interactions in the alley that gives them all the same access to the street. That connection prevents them from experiencing fully the anonymity of city life. Because there are so many yards in Lower Sainte Thérèse, the very existence of the slum may depend on the existence of those yards and vice versa. Sociologically speaking the yard constitutes one level of integration of the slum into the city and one level of adaptation of the poor to the urban scene. In the same way that a neighbourhood is a community, a yard must be seen as a microcommunity because of the interaction among the members, and also because, over the years, it may develop a distinct personality.

From the standpoint of urban development there are some observations that one can make in regard to the history of the *quartier*. The closer one's house is to the street the more likely that one is of a higher social class than other residents. The closer one's house is to the canal the more likely that one is of a social class lower than that of the other residents, and possibly a recent immigrant. The division of the space – proximity to the main street or the canal – is a reflection of one's social position and an indication of one's social class.

There is also a time factor in the settlement of the *quartier*. The earliest residents took advantage of the land close to the main street. They used their dwellings to accumulate capital by renting them to newcomers. This early pattern is repeated again with the first wave of squatters. Here the renters became squatters and exploited the land to their own advantage by renting to others. The second wave of squatters did the same. Squatterisation is one way to make money, a means to controlling and exploiting the land to one's profit. So, in the yard, one finds side by side the dwellings of owners and renters. One may think of this pattern as an hierarchisation of exploitation –

neighbours exploiting other neighbours. Such is free enterprise and the functioning of the capitalist system at the bottom of Martinican society. Eyre (1984, p. 263) has observed a similar process in the shanty towns of Jamaica. He notes that 'in all settlements which begin as capture land landlordism quickly establishes itself and capturers become rentiers in course of time'.

The position of houses in the yard is also a function of time and reflects the period over which the owners built them. For example, one would not expect front street houses to be owned by new squatters. If they are new to the *quartier*, they are more likely to be renters. Over time also some of the dwellings are transformed from wood frames to cement blocks.

Sociologically speaking the yard tends to create units whose members interact more among themselves than with others. Because of the segmentation between squatterisation and renting, one expects the house owners to establish some solidarity among themselves. The owners form the old guard, while the renters form a more transient population. The renters, especially the ones in the back yard, tend to move to better quarters as soon as they are able to do so. Territorial upward mobility is not a routine matter within the yard but is rather movement out of the yard.

We find an hierarchisation of space in the slum in general and in the yard in particular. The houses facing the main boulevard are in better condition than the ones inside the yard. The houses in the yard closer to the boulevard tend to be in better shape than the ones farther away, in the back. The maintenance of an hierarchy of place seems to be important in the reproduction of social inequality and sheds light on the process of stratification within the poor group itself. The dependency of the people in the area on the bourgeoisie tends also to be hierarchised. Those at the bottom are simply more dependent and vulnerable than the others. The reproduction of poverty in this context becomes the reproduction of that hierarchy of dependence as well.

SLUM AND SQUATTER SETTLEMENT: A STRUCTURAL MODEL OF EVOLUTION

The yard is a microspatial unit that is of some importance to an understanding of the ecology of slum life in Martinique. However, the poor are to be found not only in the slums but also in the squatter settlements such as Texaco and Volga Plage. The evolution of these neighbourhoods follows a path similar to that described by Eyre (1972) in Jamaica, which consists of four phases.[8]

The early settlement phase. In the peri-urban slum, this phase conforms to the beginning of the development of the yard. It is characterised by the acquisition of a piece of land by renting from the state and the construction of a family house or a business. The initial family may or may not live with others, but when other people are brought in, they are likely to be at the service of the family and its friends. The original yard is basically a family compound and functions through the mechanisms of kinship, solidarity, and friendship.

In the squatter settlements this phase consists of the invasion of the unoccupied public and state land by newcomers who delimit the area that is theirs and proceed to build precarious shacks. This is a period of instability, since the city can bulldoze their huts and evict them at any time. The squatters live with this constant fear. These first dwellings are not built to last, but simply to provide shelter for the time being.

The initial phase is characterised in the squatter settlements by what one may refer to as a 'survival architecture', which is different from traditional Martinican architecture or urban vernacular architecture (see also Letchimy 1984, p. 10). The urban vernacular architecture has had a long history, employs durable materials, and is intended to last a long time. It is vernacular because its style is not generic 'modern' but rather reflects the material folk culture of the island. 'Survival architecture' is for the immediate present and future, and the intent is to transform it into something more respectable once circumstances allow. For this reason such structures are composed of used wood and metal sheets that can be acquired cheaply and easily.

The expansionist phase. In the slum this is the period when the first settlers or their descendants start building new structures either to meet their own housing needs or to rent to others as a way of accumulating capital. At this time the settlers may acquire legal titles to a portion of the land, thereby leaving the rest for others to move into. The remaining portion of the land may be invaded or occupied by the initial family, by those who were renting from them, or by new squatters, that is, rural migrants.

In the squatter settlements, the second phase corresponds to that of land speculation. Part of the terrain is leased or sold to newcomers. These transactions are evidently illegal, since the land belongs to the government. This is the time when the neighbourhood takes its shape and alleys or public roads are created or marked out.

The initial modernisation phase. This corresponds to the period during which some shacks are transformed into cement block houses. As the community becomes a political force and a potential source of votes, the modernisation strategy is followed as a way of preventing the city from bulldozing the area. This is the time at which the state intervenes to provide electricity, running water, street names, and house numbers.

The integration phase. In the slum this is a slow process; in the squatter settlement integration seems to follow several years after the settlers erect their shacks. As people continue to build, less and less land is available for cultivation. During 'integration' one witnesses the vertical extension of the houses, other floors being added to the original structures (Suivant, Mora, and Fazincani 1986, p. 6). The final phase corresponds to the integration of the neighbourhood as part of the city landscape. At this time all the city services are provided, such as, for example, schools. The neighbourhood has then attained the status of part of the city landscape and is entitled to the same privileges as the other districts. The decision to integrate the slum is developed through a lengthy period of soul-searching, whereas in the case of the squatter settlements the decision is made more quickly, perhaps as a reflection of the settlers' level of organisation.

This integration effort is in conformity with the city's strategy of helping the squatter settlements as well as the slums to reproduce themselves as functional units within the city, as marginal neighbourhoods, and as dependent on the dominant sector of society. For example, the effort of building a school is put forth, in part, to provide children with a ghetto school so that they will not interfere with the schools attended by children of the bourgeois families, and also as an attempt to keep the neighbourhood free of disruptive problems. Integration is a case of engineering spatial inequality and reproducing poverty by design, however unconscious it may be. The dwellers understand that well, which is why, when they have the money, they send their children to attend school outside the neighbourhood.

DWELLERS' RESPONSES TO THE HOUSING PROBLEM

The development of the slum or the squatter settlement is the most effective response of the urban poor to their housing needs. These neighbourhoods must be seen not as problem-creating entities, but rather as responses to a problem, that is, the inability of the city to construct decent housing or even to make existing housing available to them.

It is mostly through self-help schemes that the dwellers manage to solve their housing problems. They do so through using various techniques of survival, such as the *coup-de-main*, a mechanism of exchange and solidarity through which people help each other to pursue certain goals. This solidarity is manifested especially in the construction of houses. Before departmentalisation, the *coup-de-main* was basically a rural institution. With the migration of the rural folk to Fort-de-France, the institution was to some extent urbanised. Horowitz (1967, p. 32) provides a description of the *coup-de-main* phenomenon in rural Martinique. He notes that:

> The average cultivator regularly shares his labor with a handful of fellow villagers. These labor exchange groups are called coups-de-main, composed of three to six men who cooperate in the heavy work of land-clearing and harvesting. During the appropriate seasons they work on a regular schedule, each member having a turn in sequence. Usually they work as a group for the morning only, and return to their own fields in the afternoon. Each man brings his own tools and food. The person who is receiving the day provides rum and fruit juice, and if the work lasts for the entire day, the midday meal as well.

When city dwellers decide to build a home in a lower-class neighbourhood, they may not be able to hire a builder for a fee. Rather they are likely to organise a *coup-de-main* for the construction. This consists mainly of requesting the help of friends, acquaintances, and neighbours, who may have special skills or knowledge of house building. The owner pays for the material, and carpenters, masons, electricians, and plumbers may work on weekends or occasionally during the week, free of charge. Sometimes they may even carry to the neighbourhood leftover or unused materials acquired from another, paid, job. The proprietor is asked to pay for transportation and food, but not for labour. This type of organisation consists not only of getting help from others, but also of helping others when they are in need. It is fair to say that many individuals would not have completed their houses if it were not for the help they received through the *coup-de-main*. In the late seventies Bouliane (1979, p. 55) interviewed several Volga Plage residents who were involved in the *coups-de-main* either as guests or as hosts.

In addition to building shacks on unused land for personal use or to rent to others, residents meet their housing needs in a number of ways. There are four types of housing arrangement in the neighbourhood: there are family dwellings in which the members of a nuclear family live, sometimes sharing with one or more siblings of the parents. One finds other houses used both as family dwellings and shops. Then there are rented apartments, and finally houses that are rented for the nuclear family or for use as shops. Members of the extended family may routinely live in any of these arrangements until they are able to build their own houses.

The yards of Lower Sainte Thérèse comprise a number of sets of family compounds. In the Mangatale yard there were twenty-one houses, nine of them occupied by individual families unrelated to one another through kinship ties. Among the remaining twelve houses five were inhabited by individuals of the same extented family and two more were occupied by a mother and her daughter. The number of family members still living in the Valère yard was more impressive. Out of thirty-six structures fourteen belong to the Valères and their descendants, three houses to the members of an extended family, and two more to another family. As in the yards of Lower Sainte Thérèse, people who live in the squatter settlements tend also to have family members in the neighbourhood. It was found that 45 per cent of the dwellers in Texaco, a squatter settlement in Fort-de-France, have family living there (Letchimy 1984, p. 85). In the slum and squatter settlements of Fort-de-France, some individuals own their houses, others rent from landlords who live side by side with them, and still others rent from property-owners who live in other neighbourhoods.

REPRODUCTION OF POVERTY

Poverty tends to breed in a structural environment that hinders the growth of individual and community. The slums and squatters settlements of Fort-de-France provide such a niche. By focusing on their mode of incorporation and interaction with the city we may acquire a better idea of the mechanisms that sustain urban poverty.

The overview and the data given above show the hierarchy of environments and resources in the city. The urban space is divided up into areas of inequality where the poor have access neither in their home nor in the neighbourhoods to the resources that could encourage their upward mobility. This allocation of space is a causal factor in the reproduction of poverty. As Peet (1975, p. 564) notes, 'Inequality may be passed on from one generation to the next via the environment of opportunities and services into which each individual is implanted at birth'. The slum and the squatter settlement constitute niches of inequality in the city and are conducive to the reproduction of poverty among their inhabitants.

Poverty is reproduced in the slum and in the squatter settlement because the workers have never received the market value of their labour, and because the services offered in their neighbourhoods never reflect a reasonable return on their contributions to the state. They are exploited individually because they receive salaries below the value of their labour and as a class because their neighbourhoods are not given the services provided to other segments of society.

The lower-class neighbourhoods constitute a labour pool. Attracted to the city in search of employment the inhabitants remain in the slums and provide their services to the government and the business community. Workers from the slums are found everywhere and clearly help keep the wheels of the city turning. Those who are unemployed or underemployed constitute a reserve pool of cheap labour.

The neighbourhoods are also markets for the local economy. They consume goods either from the business district or from the neighbourhood stores, and no doubt many businesses are geared toward that market. Those businesses depend on their consumption capabilities.

The interaction of the lower-class neighbourhoods with the rest of the city can be seen also from the standpoint of monetary circulation. The informal economy, which also sustains the formal economy, is a means of survival used by the poor. The money made in the informal economy may be invested in the formal economy. It is evident that those who function in the informal sector are likely to make less profit than those who work in the formal sector.

The landlords in the slums and squatter settlements make a good deal of money from renting their dwellings to the poor. They are able to do so because of their knowledge of the housing market, and of the needs and capabilities of their clients. The poor do not have the contacts to find space to rent in nicer neighbourhoods and often do not have the steady incomes necessary to do so. They are forced to rent substandard housing from landlords who rely on this income for their own subsistence and for the accumulation of capital.

Once they reach the slum or squatter settlement the newcomers will socialise only with lower-class people. Thus the possibility of upward mobility is hindered in two ways. On the one hand, they do not have the proper contacts, and therefore access to the necessary information, to do well. On the other hand, because of daily expenditures for themselves and their dependants, they are not always able to save. The situation may worsen if they go through cyclical periods of unemployment.

The slum or the squatter settlement reproduces poverty because the people in its midst suffer from both unemployment and underemployment. Both categories maintain the dwellers at a level at which they are unable to improve their way of life. They therefore develop a series of strategies through the informal sector of the economy and the solidarity mechanisms, which help them cope with everyday life but not necessarily in the accumulation of capital.

The slum reproduces poverty because the state either does not care much about the poor who live there or does not translate its concern into a genuine and sustained effort to eradicate the causes of the slum. State interventions through various allocations tend to maintain the poor at the threshold of poverty. Poverty is reproduced not simply because the poor lack imagination and opportunities, but because the state fails to help them escape from the situation.

This chapter has tried to shed light on three correlated issues. One, the dominant sector of society controls the distribution of the urban space and influences the hierarchisation of locations. Two, the reproduction of poverty is made possible in poor neighbourhoods because of the asymmetrical relations between inhabitants and their employers and also because they find themselves at the bottom of the hierarchy of environments. Third, dwellers do not have real access to resources and meaningful social contacts within their environment, as other social classes do.

NOTES

1.   For an elaboration of the early development of Fort-de-France during the colonial era, see the following: Memoirs 1700, 1761, 1816. Letchimy (1984, p. 7) argues that the site of the city was selected because of the advantages it offered: the security of the bay for the defence of the colony, its central geographical position in regard to the colonisation of

hinterland, and its location for maritime commercial traffic in terms of port activities. Two books now available on the general history of Fort-de-France are Relouzat (1968) and Janin (1924).

2. For a detailed study of the main market by an urban geographer, see the master's thesis by Glondu (1983). The public markets are not the only places where vendors sell their products. Those who operate in the informal sector of the economy also sell their products in other locations in the city. Letchimy (1984, p. 128) notes that 'le petit commerce de détail se caractérise aussi à la périphérie du centre par la présence de marchands ambulants pratiquant la revente de produits alimentaires (poissons, légumes) et non-alimentaires (bijoux, produits artisanaux). Au centreville ils s'installent dans des véhicules adaptés à cet effet et participent activement à l'animation de nuit dans certains secteurs. Les vendeurs d'eau de coco sont certainement les plus nombreux et les plus dynamiques de ces commerçants informels. Après avoir fait la cueillette de cocos dans tous les coins de l'île, ils se rendent sur l'une des places fréquentées de la ville, munis de leurs coutelas, pour vendre.'

3. On the meaning of the 'cinquante pas géométriques', see the excellent study by ADUAM (1980). Letchimy (1985, p. 133) defines it as 'le domaine privé de l'Etat mis en place sous l'ancien régime et maintenu dans les DOM, il représente une bande de terrain de 81, 20 mètres à partir de la ligne naturelle du rivage'.

4. Martinique became a Department of France on 19 March 1946. For a historical sketch of the history of Martinique from 1635 to 1946 see Achéen (1983, 1815–1935).

5. This corroborates an earlier observation by Petit-Mau. In his description of la Cour Clindor, he notes 'Située à 800 mètres du Grand Marché; à 400 mètres de l'église . . ., c'est à son premier locataire . . . qu'elle doit son appellation. Les gens du quartier disaient communément "la cour où habite Mme Clindor", puis "la Cour Madame Clindor" et la "Cour Clindor"' (Petit-Mau 1947, p. 12).

6. This economic aspect is also stressed by Petit-Mau. He wrote that after the death of Mme Clindor, there were forty-five rooms, in la Cour Clindor, inhabited by thirty-six couples and eighty single individuals. The great majority of them were tenants (Petit-Mau 1947, p. 13).

7. For the history or a description of these yards, see Anon (1970), Petit-Mau (1947), Pamphile (1985a). The Cour Fruit à Pain no longer exists. A description of the area where it was located is provided by an anonymous writer: 'Au droit de la Route Nationale No. 3, au départ de Fort-de-France, conduit vers Balata, on aperçoit, avant d'atteindre le Pond-de-Chaines, un quartier occupé par des constructions hétéroclites . . . . Ce quartier qui couvre une superficie 23000m^2 forme une avancée de l'agglomération des Terres-Sainville, entre la Rivière Madame et le Canal de Trénelle.'

8. This model is an adaptation of an earlier one developed by geographer Alan Eyre (1972, pp. 401–2) in regard to the development of the shantytowns of Montego Bay, Jamaica.

3 The Urban Household as a Multi-Product Firm

Any attempt at explaining urban poverty in the Caribbean in general and in Martinique in particular must at some point focus on the lower-class household or the extended family. It is the 'factory' where poverty is reproduced both on an everyday basis and transgenerationally. It is the family unit that has the power to help its members, to some degree, wage constant war against the several forms of material poverty they may experience. Scrutiny on the household as the locus of the reproduction of poverty is important on two grounds. On the one hand, the household functions as a microinstitutional basis of the reproduction of poverty and is the repository of the strategies that people develop to solve their problems. Second, such scrutiny reveals the structural constraints, generated by the wider system, that may have a direct impact on the failure or success of the struggle to overcome the burden of poverty. That second aspect will not be addressed fully here because it will require a sharper focus on the political economy of Martinique and on the ecology of state policies and politics.

In the previous studies of lower-class black families in the United States and the Caribbean, five methodological and theoretical approaches have been proposed. One thinks of Herskovits's cultural continuity model, which views the organisations of the black family in the new world as truncated forms of West African practices (Herskovits, 1941); Frazier's non-marxian class analysis linking the matrifocality phenomenon to the marginal position of the black man in the political economy of the United States (Frazier, 1939); Smith's developmental cycle model, which stresses the phases the household goes through during its life history (Smith, 1956); Shimkin's and colleagues' extended family approach, which views the household as one node in a network of relationships with other households (Shimkin et al., 1978). Each one of these models has clarified some aspects of the organisation of the lower-class black family. Oscar Lewis's 'culture of poverty' could also be pertinent to this inquiry, since it is a counterpart to the argument presented here (Lewis, 1966). His emphasis on pathologies, although it is useful in many different ways in understanding the plight of the poor, has its own shortcomings.

50

Valentine (1968) pointed up the fallacy of Lewis's reasoning, and Stack has provided a systematic and empirical rebuttal to Lewis, arguing that 'the life ways of the poor present a powerful challenge to the notion of self-perpetuating culture of poverty' (Stack, 1975, p. 129).

In this chapter the lower-class urban Martinican household will be studied as a special kind of business venture, a multiproduct firm.[1] The rationale of this approach is that once the mechanisms that explain the functioning of the firms are identified we will be in a better position to understand the process of social reproduction: the reproduction of the division of labour within the unit, the reproduction of the 'breadwinner power' and the reproduction of the asymmetric relationships between the household and the dominant sector of society. All these 'departments' of reproduction are tightly linked to each other and to the working of the state economy.

Business firms, like other socioeconomic units in society, go through some evolutionary changes. It is worth recalling here the four stages that characterise the process of evolution or the complex organisational forms of the firm. Thompson (1973, pp. 24–7) identifies

a state I enterprise as a one-man management show where the owner-entrepreneur has close daily contact with each employee and each phase of operations . . . . The firm's strengths, vulnerabilities, and resources are closely allied with the entrepreneur's personality, management ability and style, and personal financial situation.

From an organisational standpoint, state II firms differ from state I enterprises in one essential respect: an increased scale, scope and complexity of operations make management specialization imperative and force a transition from one-man management to group management.

The third stage includes those organizations whose operations, though concentrated in a single field or product line, are large enough and scattered over a wide enough geographical area to justify having geographically decentralized units.

The fourth stage of corporate development is typified by large, multiproduct, multiplant, multimarket enterprises. Diversification and decentralized management are their distinctive features.

Clearly, when one speaks of the household as a firm, one does not mean that it is identical to any one of the forms mentioned above. The family household is a peculiar type of firm, and when seen from this angle, it appears in three different ways. The following accounts by two informants help to clarify this notion of Martinican family organisation.

> When my man died he left me with three children. We have been renting our place ever since we came to the city. Since he was the one who paid the bill and I have not been working for a while, I found myself suddenly without a source of income to pay the rent. My sister who works as a clerk at City Hall and who is the godmother of my oldest daughter has been helping me financially a great deal with the hardship I had to go through [Informant from Sainte Thérèse]
>
> I have one brother and a sister. My brother lives in Paris and comes to visit us once in a while. My sister lives in Sainte Marie. She is married and her husband has a good job. She could help me if I need her to do so. You see I am a school teacher and my husband has his own bus. I am pretty close to my sister. She does things for me and I do the same for her. On weekends, she either babysits for me or I babysit for her. [Informant from Volga Plage]

First, the household may depend almost exclusively on its own resources to transform into or maintain itself as a viable institution; the ties it maintains with other households may be more beneficial to the latter than to the former, economically speaking. There are cases in Fort-de-France in which one household is doing well and so is called to help another household in the same extended family that is undergoing financial hardship. The relationships may be less asymmetric when seen from a moral standpoint, since of course people in the same family are expected to help each other.

Second, the household may function in a symmetrical relationship with the other households. Here each household will have attained the same social and financial status, and each household may help, collaborate with, and advise the other routinely. The success of each household depends on interhousehold solidarity and commitment.

Third, the household may be unable to step over the threshold from poverty to financial stability. It depends on a parent-household for help. This is the situation of the household that not only develops its own strategies to face or solve its problems, but also is receiving financial aid and strategic advice for long- and short-term planning from another household. Its success or survival may eventually depend on this outside help. The reproduction of poverty is made possible because of the contribution of a parent-household and the household itself to its own survival.

The three forms of household arrangement previously mentioned represent different modes of relationship to other households. One should not however conclude that the relationships are intrinsic to the formulation of the urban household as a multiproduct firm. They are simply modalities that the household takes in prospecting for survival. Here again, economics tends to be the major factor in explaining the form of relationship a household may maintain over time with others.

The household as an economic unit tends to maximise revenues and minimise cost and, in the case of family enterprises, to maximise profit as well. As a viable unit of production, the household depends for its success on the availability of human capital, physical capital, and time. Here time is conceived of as a budget item and must be taken into consideration as part of the overall strategy for revenue maximisation.

In the same way that firms disintegrate, and former employees and employers join other firms or form their own, households also disintegrate and, in the process, individuals join another household (the married daughter, for example, who returns to live with her mother) or form new households (the wife who divorces her husband, for example, to marry another man).

The point to be made is that the behaviour of the household is in many ways similar to that of the firm and that the organisation of the firm is an outgrowth of the organisation of the family.[2] The microeconomic literature has clarified the many stages of development of the firm from family enterprise to corporate business; however, what is not clear is the similarity of organisation between the two. A full comparison of these units is not the purpose of the chapter. However, study of the household can be facilitated by following the economic rationale of the firm. The same external and internal factors (government policies, external market conditions, poor managerial skills) that may lead the ordinary firm to bankruptcy can be just as detrimental to the well-functioning of the household.

It should be understood at the outset that when one speaks of the household as a firm, one does not necessarily refer to family firms or enterprises. The latter are concrete business ventures operated and managed by members of a family instead of a group of shareholders or a board of directors. The notion of the household as a firm, although it may include this formal business aspect, is more inclusive and tends to view the household as an operational unit in search of the full realisation of its potential.

Although the functioning of the household shares certain features with other firms, such as risk-taking, competition, division of labour, hierarchy of positions, stage of development, motivation of actors, production, profit maximisation, investment, supply and demand, and cost minimisation, it has its own dynamics: it is after all a family first, a firm second.

Firms behave differently depending on their make-up, internal organisation, target market, and basic goals. No doubt the household is not a perfect duplicate of any of the several models of firms discussed in the microeconomic literature. It is however a firm on its own merits, and it is worthwhile defining its parameters.

By multiproduct firm I mean to suggest the diversity of the household's output and of its strategies to maximise its chance for survival and to minimise its possibility of default. It is not my purpose to reduce the household solely to an economic entity, but rather to study the unit from the standpoint of its economic goals, whether conscious or unconscious.

The notion of the household as a multiproduct firm expresses the diversity of its output. The household may end by selling more than one product; and it does not rely only on one individual for its survival. Diversity of production is here a complementary factor. A man may be engaged in doing outside work while the woman is engaged in domestic work to sustain the man and the rest of the household. The diversity of the output is to minimise risks and to allow more flexibility in the management of the household.

As in the case of any firm, the success of a household depends on its adjustment to external market and non-market conditions. It is proper to say that these external conditions influence the shape of the household as well, including the structure of the relations it maintains with the larger system.

INTERNAL ORGANISATION

In order to meet its goals, the household must have its own hierarchical structure. No doubt local cultural traditions count for something in shaping the content of individual relations in that structure. Like all firms individuals are called to play specific roles to further the aims of the enterprise, and a framework for the decision-making process is worked out, ensuring an orderly chain of command from top to bottom. Mincer and Polachek (1974, p. 397) note that 'the behavior of the household unit implies a division of labor within it. Broadly speaking, this division of labor or "differentiation of roles" emerges because the attempts to promote household life are necessarily constrained by complementarity and substitution relations in the household production process and by comparative advantages due to differential skills and earning powers with which household members are endowed'.

An informant from Volga Plage provides some clues to the dynamics of the internal organisation of the urban Martinican family-household:

> Ever since I came to live in Volga Plage, I have been doing two jobs. Since I am away for most of the time, my wife takes care of the small children and the management of the household. I have a job with the mayor's office and in the evenings and weekends I am self-employed as a fisherman. Whatever I take my wife sells it to neighbours and other acquaintances. We also eat a lot of fish, which reduces the cost of our food consumption . . . . I am not a good cook. When my lady is sick or in Sainte Anne visiting with her old relatives, my older daughter cooks for us. She is not as good at it as her mother.

The breadwinner in the household, husband or wife or both, is an entrepreneur or a capitalist with the clear goal of maximising revenue for the sake of the household. He or she goes out to work and shares his or her income with the household. In order to maximise this income, the breadwinner may participate in both the formal and informal sectors of the economy, especially if the wife is not working for a salary.

If the wife is not working outside the household for a salary, she is generally in charge of the house, which is, in the vocabulary of the firm, a managerial job in the sense that it entails responsibility over the personnel (children and husband), budgetary decisions (running the household, since most of the decisions about household expenses at this level are made by her), and providing middle-range direction and assessment.[3] When she works outside the household for a salary, she participates in more than one arena in the running of the household. She becomes both a *de facto* and *de jure* manager. Her participation in the workplace no doubt helps to reshape the structure of the decision-making process at the level of the family-household, in that it may cause an adjustment in previous asymmetric relations between partners.

Children, although they may be economically dependent on their parents, also play a positive role in the management of this kind of firm. They help with household chores, and their presence may enhance the happiness of the family-household and give it a sense of direction. From this angle the reality of the household as a firm is more pronounced when there are children than when there are not.

As the children grow older and start making money, they may contribute to the household revenues. Sometimes they contribute their expertise, such as helping parents with legal advice, or in other ways, as through their manual skills or their contacts. The financial role of children is more pronounced in the context of household enterprises. They help in several ways with the running of the enterprise, even to the extent of taking over the management of the household business venture at a certain age.

In the hierarchy of positions within the household a fundamental point remains the flexibility and interchangeability of roles, which is essential to ensure the success of the firm. Here I am referring to the willingness and ability of members occasionally to shift roles, as for example, when the father babysits so as to allow the mother to run an errand, or a son manages the household business while the father is sick or out of town. Over the years the members of the household will have learned to play one another's roles.

The internal organisation of the household is a clear example of the fact that the reproduction of a system means the reproduction of its hierarchical components. In the case of the family, I refer more specifically to the division of labour and the ability, for example, to reproduce the breadwinner's position in the system. Such hierarchical roles do not have their own autonomy; rather they are produced as part of the asymmetric relationship of the household with society.

A DECISION-MAKING UNIT

A householder from Sainte Thérèse had the following to say about day-to-day decision making:

> The small decisions concerning the running of the household are left to my wife. She does not like me to tell her what to cook every day and what kinds of clothes she should buy for the children. I give her some money and she tells me what she is going to use it for. Likewise she is not interested in knowing how I manage to invite

acquaintances to help me build the house. I make those decisions. Sometimes we discuss matters together before we take a decision. For example, last year, I wanted to send my boy to a private school and she was convinced that it was better to use the money for my older daughter to go to Paris. She thought that was the best way to separate her from her boyfriend and free her mind so that she can learn something in school. So, she is now attending school in Paris.

When we look at the household as a decision-making unit, we see that it is actively engaged in evaluative thinking about getting the best for its members. Goals are set consciously or unconsciously, long-term and short-term. However, the achievement of these goals may be hindered for any number of reasons: because, for example, the decision-maker's expectations are unrealistic even under optimal conditions, or because he or she is unable to devise effective methods toward those ends. The achievement of goals may also be burdened by situational contexts that constrain and limit their realisation. External factors, include, for example, government policies. Once these variables are identified the components that make up aspects of the reproduction of poverty are better understood.

Reid (1934, p. 77) pinpoints with accuracy the function of the household as a decision-making unit. She notes that

> management in the household consists largely of: 1) choice-making, that is, deciding what specific goods will best meet the needs and desires of the members of the household; 2) income apportionment, involving decisions as to the use of money income; 3) taste and time apportionment, including decisions as to the use of cooperation of household members, the assignment to various members of tasks to be performed, and the arranging of these in the time sequence desired; 4) the planning of ways and means of carrying on household tasks, which involves finding satisfactory methods for specific tasks, and in many cases presents economic, technical, and esthetic problems; and 5) the actual direction of the household which includes giving orders and supervising the work of others.

The household makes decisions every day, sometimes of strategic importance, some others of a more trivial nature. These are individual or collective (corporate) decisions that may engage one or more people in the unit. In the household there may be a specialisation in the decision-making process. Some individuals, because of their responsibilities in the running of the household, may make decisions concerning specific activities. Some decisions are short-range, others long-range. There are mechanisms through which previous decisions are reassessed and new ones are made. This means a decision taken by one person can be overturned or overruled by another or by the group, once better information emerges.

Families make decisions concerning their consumption patterns, the use of their time, their general expenses, their leisure or productive activities, and so on. It is clear that families decide on the number of children they wish to have in consideration of their desired life-style and of what they expect from their offspring. They make decisions concerning the kind of education they want for their children and about where they want their children to go to school. In Martinique the choice is between private and public schools or between Martinican schools and emigration to metropolitan France. Furthermore the household constantly evaluates its budget to bring it in line with its consumption and other expenses. Some expenses found to be unnecessary (or even necessary, but not essential) may be curtailed. They also evaluate their time, which they divide into communal household activities, household chores, outside labour, recreational activity, worship, and individual free time. These decisions may not be explicit, but they are part of the general operation of the household.

In the absence of a boardroom it is around the dinner table (or in the bedroom) that husband and wife talk informally about formal business affairs. They discuss, for example, matters pertaining to the running of the household. This is one of the reasons why the children often find adult conversation rather boring and do not want to take part.

The function of the decision-making process here is to articulate the household to the rest of society. Although, theoretically speaking, the residents are free to make decisions on their own, in practice they are entangled in a web of relationships that reduce their freedom. These decisions, because they are made for the survival of the family, can also at times be contributing factors in the reproduction of poverty.

A UNIT OF PRODUCTION

The production factor is a major aspect in the operation of the household. The success of a household depends on its ability to produce sufficient income for the well-being of the family. Most of the members may be involved directly or indirectly in the production process. The inability to produce leads to the daily reproduction of poverty in that household. The following account by an informant from Volga Plage, gives us a glimpse of the production process at the household level. 'You ask me how do we make money to run the household. It is not simple . . . . I work as a docker. That's my job. But from time to time, being a mason, I work for clients in my free time. My wife is a vendor at the public market. We also have another source of income – that little house over there which we rent to a Haitian couple.'

Production is defined here in terms of 'any activity which creates value' (Thompson, 1973, p. 180). The everyday life of the household depends on the ability of its members to produce goods, places to rent, income, and time. As Mincer and Polachek (1974, p. 397) note, 'the household is viewed as an economic unit which shares consumption and allocates production at home and in the market as well as the investments in physical and human capital of its members'. While the household continues to consume, it must generate an income to pay for these expenses. The way in which households produce income varies from one to another. There are three basic means of production in the household: (1) self-employment as an integral part of the household, by way for example, of a household enterprise such as a farm; (2) providing services to others, as in the case of renting a room in one's house; or (3) employment by others, such as work in external firms. In the three instances above, goods, skills, and services useful to the household or saleable to others are the products. For Reid (1934, p. 11) household production of the first type consists of 'those unpaid activities which are carried on, by and for the members, which activities might be replaced by market goods, or paid services, if circumstances such as income, market conditions, and personal inclinations permit the service being delegated to someone outside the household group'. In the second and third category, one sells one's labour and one's expertise in return for an income.

In the slum of Sainte Thérèse and the squatter settlement of Volga Plage we find grocery shops owned by local residents. Such shops are frequently the only way or the chief way these families can generate income. Grocery shops provide permanent employment for members of the household, and the profits they accrue are the economic basis of the household. All the adult members of the household participate in the running of the shop – in the acquisition and transportation of goods, bookkeeping, selling, and managing the store. Other households produce crafts or run barber-shops, thereby providing services to the community for a fee.

Among the self-employed we must distinguish between those who work in the formal sector of the economy and those who work in the informal sector. By formal sector I mean all those economic activities that are known to the state and for which the worker or entrepreneur pays taxes. The informal sector refers to activities that are not so regulated by the state.

The majority of the slum inhabitants work for outside institutions in the private and public sectors. Production here means the income they produce by selling their time, expertise, or labour. In a given household there may be more than one person engaged in the production process. The notion of corporate productivity as a form of family organisation is not unique to households in the urban centres of Martinique. Horowitz (1967, p. 39), who did his field work earlier in rural Martinique, found that 'a household includes those persons who habitually reside in the same structure and who have a common fund for consumptive use' and that 'corporate productivity, particularly in farming and marketing, is a frequent but not necessary condition for the unit'.

As a unit of production, the household like any other firm makes decisions about what goods and services it wants to produce for itself and what it prefers to buy from others. These decisions are often made in terms of cost minimisation and the time it takes to produce such goods. When buying goods and services is evaluated as being less costly than producing them, the household prefers to buy them. When it is more costly to buy, the household is likely to produce them. Becker (1976, p. 106) notes that 'instead of travelling to a shop, waiting in line, receiving a shave and continuing to another destination, men now shave themselves at home saving travelling, waiting and even some shaving time . . . . The movement of shaving from barbers' shops to households illustrates how and why even in urban areas households have become 'small factories'.

A UNIT OF CONSUMPTION

It is through consumption that the household subsists and continues to function. Indeed, without consumption, the household could not reproduce itself. The testimony of an informant who lives in Volga Plage illustrates the constant pressing nature of family consumption.

As I told you, we cannot save money. Life has become so expensive in Fort-de-France. While I was in Sainte Anne, I could rely on my garden for vegetables and other food products. Here I must buy everything that we eat. In addition, I pay the rent each month and for my son who is attending a private school. To live here one has to pay a lot of money. This why I do a great deal of calculation before I waste my money on anything I may buy.

Consumption is an important consideration in the present elaboration of the household as a multiproduct firm. It has been proved, on the basis of research carried out in the United States, that 'consumption behavior represents mainly joint household or household decisions rather than separate decisions of household members' (Mincer and Polachek 1974, p. 391). Consumption is of primary interest to this study because it is one of the areas in the functioning of the household that sheds light on the reproduction of poverty. Dickinson and Russell (1986, p. 9) found that 'the family-household appears as the primary institution of individual consumption and hence, in turn, is also the societal locus of generational reproduction through legitimate procreation, child bearing and initial socialization. Importantly, in a capitalist economy, this sphere appears to the worker as an island of self-determination in an otherwise very large ocean of externally-manifested hierarchical power and discipline relations.'

In the running of the household there are seven types of costs that must be kept under control. (1) *Daily consumption costs*, which include food and drink, are a biological necessity to keep the members in good shape. (2) *Medical costs*, which refer both to actual medical expenses and to insurance is expenditure to maintain good health. (3) *Leisure costs*, referring to individual and household entertainment that must be paid out of the household budget. (4) *Operational costs*, which refer to the structural aspects in the maintenance of a household, such as the upkeep of the house, the yard or the car. (5) *Educational costs*, which entail expenses incurred for the education of children. (6) *Social costs*, which arise because the family must interact in society: examples are buying clothes and offering gifts. (7) *Religious costs*, the amount of money one gives to a church or to a church-sponsored charitable organisation.

As a household makes plans in advance of expenditure, each one of these categories is juggled against the revenue in order not to go under. In the management of the household there is a continual adjustment to actual and projected cost so that the money that is set aside for one category is not used for another one. However this diversion can be made when it is necessary to do so.

A UNIT OF DISTRIBUTION

In order to ensure its survival, the household may engage in the development of a family enterprise. However, its ability to succeed in such a venture may depend on the ability to accumulate some capital for the welfare of the household. To achieve that goal the household may serve as a distribution unit. Failure to use this strategy may also contribute to the inability to run the business, and eventually to poverty. A shop owner in Sainte Thérèse describes how his family shares in running their enterprise: 'We have been managing this grocery shop for seven years. My oldest son has a car; sometimes we ask him to take the merchandise we buy from the wholesale place and bring it here. The other day an older client was not feeling well and my daughter was passing by her house; she asked her to buy some butter for her, since my daughter was going to the downtown, my wife took it to her.' Another shopkeeper, this one from Volga Plage, tells how the business spills over into the household: 'The room that we are using for our grocery shop is small. I can seldom put everything we have in it. These are a box of soap and another of oil that I store in the bedroom. Things that I cannot put on display immediately usually I place them in another room.'

When a household is used as a base of operation for a family enterprise, it serves as a distribution unit. To minimise cost, members of the household take part in the distribution and transportation of goods from wholesalers to the household enterprise and sometimes from there to a public market or a client's house.

As a distribution unit, the household provides both transportation and storage, which if done by others would be provided for a fee. By using its own members and its own household space to store merchandise or products the household is able to lower its operational cost and maximise its revenue.

PROFIT MAXIMISATION

In every human economic enterprise profit is a goal to be achieved. In its overall operation the household, in part simply to avoid catastrophic penury, behaves no differently. How a small family business works for profit is related by an informant in Volga Plage.

> This *boutique* is a small operation. It is nothing like the big stores run by the Béké in downtown Fort-de-France or the textile stores run by the Syrians on Arago Street. The store simply helps my family get by. I certainly make a profit; if not I would not still be around. I buy from the wholesale place and sell on a retail basis. I do not make much, but enough to send the children to a private school.

In the words of Thompson (1973, p. 310) 'profit is . . . the entrepreneur's compensation and reward for fulfilling his economic and managerial functions successfully. Losses are the penalty for entrepreneurial failure.'

Economic profit, including accounting or normal profit, is calculated as the differential between total revenue and total cost ($\pi = tr - tc$). The cost of running a household enterprise when subtracted from the total revenue provides the profit. It is evident that much effort is expended to reduce cost so as to maximise profit. In the case of individuals who work for an outside institution, the strategy followed is to reduce costs so as to bring more money home.

Even when applied to the firm, the profit-maximisation model has its limitations. As Hawkins (1973, p. 7) puts it, 'Unfortunately the theory of the firm is currently in a state of considerable confusion. Many economists are dissillusioned with profit-maximization models but are not yet able to agree on a generally acceptable alternative theory. . . . All intuition suggests utility maximization as the "right" alternative to profit maximization." I use the term "profit" here for lack of a better one to express the kind of reward and compensation that the family looks to get in return for a successful management of a household. When I speak of the Martinican household trying 'to maximize its profit', I do not refer exclusively to monetary profits or benefits. Social and human benefits must also be included.

REVENUE MAXIMISATION

Revenue maximisation is an antidote to poverty. A resident of Volga Plage explains how he and his wife were able to maximise the revenue of their household.

When my wife was pregnant she used to make dresses for our neighbours. She had a good clientele. She used the money she made to buy clothes for our baby. For the past ten years, she has been working at the general hospital and on weekends she continues to fix dresses for her clients. I work for the government, but being a carpenter I also make a little bit of extra money whenever someone requests my services. If we have not been saving and making money, there is no way we could have built that house.

It is clearly the wish of every household to bring as much money home as possible. Strategies are developed to capture the largest possible revenues. This is certainly true in the case of those who run a household enterprise. Those who are employed by others will also work hard to achieve greater earnings, and the reasons for such revenue maximisation are often spelled out in terms of the welfare of the household or the achievement of a goal.

It is in correlation with a projected household life-style that the concept of revenue maximisation must be understood. To maximise the revenue of the household more than one person may be asked to or may choose to work. If possible the household may even rent an apartment or dwelling to another person as supplemental earning, which can be permanent, transitory, or cyclical. The maximum revenue of the household is the result of the total addition of the income of every member, plus the services provided for unpaid household work. However, not all the money earned by members of the household is made available to cover the expenses incurred. Men may spend part of their income to keep girlfriends in the city. At the same time one may also say that the maximum revenue of a household includes as well money given by boyfriends or sent by relatives who live in metropolitan France.

COST MINIMISATION

I prefer to speak of 'costs' in general terms, because the term cannot be easily defined. Reid (1934, p. 160) notes that 'costs in household production have three outstanding characteristics: first, it is difficult, if not impossible, to estimate many of them in monetary terms; second, it is difficult to determine the direct cost of separate goods and services; and third, many of the costs are indirect, or overhead.'

Whether one looks at the household from the standpoint of profit maximisation or revenue maximisation, or both, it becomes evident that cost minimisation is also a goal to be achieved. In the running of a household there is a clear desire to keep cost down in order to have enough control over the budget and to maintain the largest margin possible between expenses and revenue. For example, consumption is maintained in line globally not necessarily item by item. Without a constant effort at minimising the cost of running the household, this could lead to poverty. The following strategies are used by a lower income Martinican household. 'Our monthly income has not changed that much for the past two years' says the informant, a resident of Volga Plage. 'But, as you can see the price of almost everything has gone up. We have been very careful about our expenses. For example, we try to buy things when they are on sale. We buy more food products from the supermarkets because they tend to be a bit cheaper than from our neighbourhood boutiques.'

OVERHEADS

Schultz (1974, p. 8) provides a most revealing perspective on the meaning of overheads in the context of household organisation. He states that 'the household as a decision-making unit with respect to household production is here viewed as an application of the theory of the firm in traditional economic theory. In this view of the household, the assumption is made that the welfare of each member of the household is normally integrated into a unified household welfare function, that there are "overheads", and that shadow (non-market) prices play an important role in the family's producer and consumer activities, including the bearing and rearing of children.'

A certain balance is sought between revenue and overheads. When overheads take too large a bite from the revenue of the household, it becomes a cause of concern, because this is the path that leads to poverty. Such is particularly the case of those who instead of saving by living in affordable housing use much of their revenue to pay the monthly rent. Unless they make some readjustment, that style of living will become troublesome for them.

Not everyone in the family may work for a salary. The housewife who takes care of the children and cooks for the rest of the family is sometimes unable to; however, she pursues activities that are essential if the breadwinner is to function as such. For that reason those who are employed and receive a salary pay overheads for the maintenance and running of the household; for example, children may be asked to return a portion of their salaries to help defray the expenses of the household. Overheads are given in terms of cash but also in terms of labour and time. The housewife thus provides her non-remunerated labour as part of what is needed to pay the overheads.

INVESTMENT

One of the characteristic goals of the family-household is to invest in the future. Investment is a strategy used by the household as a way out of poverty. The survival of the household as a kinship unit may be attributable in part to its ability to invest in whatever can produce a return. Investment, here, must not be seen exclusively in monetary terms. To place money in a bank to save for the future, to buy a house or a piece of land, is an investment in physical capital.

People also invest in human capital. For example, a household may decide to have children in the hope that they will take care of the parents in their old age. For Willis (1974, p. 27) 'the motives for having children may include both the direct satisfaction children are expected to provide their parents and the indirect satisfaction they may render by working in the household or household business or by remitting money income to their parents. Thus, fertility is motivated by consumption, saving, or investment considerations.' Schultz (1974, p. 6) elaborates on the same idea when he writes that 'children are here viewed as forms of human capital . . . . In poor countries children . . . contribute substantially to the future real income of their parents by the work that children do in the household and on the farm and by the food and shelter they provide for their parents when they no longer are able to provide these for themselves. Children are in a very important sense the poor man's capital.'

Families invest in education so that the children will have the necessary skills to do well later, when, it is understood, they will be able to help themselves and repay their parents. Money spent on education thus is not lost, but is invested.

Sometimes families invest in other people as well. They may help others by offering them gifts and providing them with services. To the extent that this is done in the hope of receiving something in return (friends, for example, or a good reputation because of one's act of charity), such generosity can be viewed as an investment in social capital. Sometimes one helps someone else in order to be able to ask that person a favour later.

A CREDIT UNIT

The family-household operates also as a credit unit. It both gives and takes credit. Giving credit is in itself an investment in social capital. One gives a loan to someone in the hope of getting a loan from that person when in need, or simply to maintain an ongoing relationship. Giving credit without interest may also be a factor in the reproduction of poverty. It is a solidarity mechanism that may hinder one's ability to use one's capital so as to accumulate a profit.

The neighbour's household or a friend is the third source of access to cash that the Martinican poor have in addition to the bank and the *sousou*. The informal arrangements by which neighbours lend and receive money with no payment of interest are necessary when the household has exhausted its credit line at a formal bank and is unable to get immediate cash from the informal rotating credit association known as *sousou*. Getting a loan may be crucial at some point for the survival of the household as a unit, and not only a loan of money. Credit can also be given in terms of services and foods to others. A household may borrow a couple of eggs or spices from a neighbour. If there are more visitors in a household than chairs, for example, it is likely that these will be borrowed from a neighbour.

TRANSFERS WITHIN THE HOUSEHOLD

Intrahousehold transfer is a strategy or mechanism whereby money, goods, and services may pass from one hand to another. It is part of the solidarity that is supposed to bind the members of the same household together. It can be seen also as an adaptation to poverty, especially as it is used by poor families.

In the Martinican household transfers of money occur between parents and children and vice-versa. Brothers and sisters help each other in time of need. It is important to see these transfers as means of maintaining the unity and integrity of the household.

Reid (1974, p. 157) notes that 'households are multiproduct firms with an exchange system within them and function in response to market and external non-market relationships'. Because of external constraints it sometimes happens that money that was allocated for one member is used to meet the needs of another member. Take the case of the money that has been saved to pay for the schooling of one member, but is reallocated to pay the medical expenses of another. On a lesser scale an informant from Volga Plage recalls that when his son,

Pierre, was a teenager, 'he used to give the pants that did not fit him well to his younger brother, Claude. And we bought him new ones. As you know, children grow up sometimes very fast.'

HOUSEHOLD-TO-HOUSEHOLD TRANSFERS

In the relations of households to one another a good deal of sharing is manifest among them at several levels.[4] That sharing has the immediate effect of reducing the burden of poverty for some. Services may be shared, as when one household helps another one to repair a house, or watches the children. The household with a car may at times do errands for the one without a car. One household may offer goods to another, or may give or receive gifts of money or loans. Children may be shared by spending time in different households where their parents reside separately. Residents will occasionally go to another home, household, or neighbour for shelter; and food is shared whenever one is invited to eat a meal in someone else's home.

The many levels of sharing or interhousehold transfers are fundamental characteristics of the lower-class Martinican household, but they constitute also a regular feature of the middle and upper-class Martinican household. The following examples illustrate the kind of transfers referred to.

The first case is a bourgeois household with three individuals: the head, who happens to be a woman, her daughter, and a housekeeper (see Table 3.1). The figure below shows for a week in July 1985 how often each member was invited to eat a meal in a friend's or relative's home.

TABLE 3.1   *Interhousehold Transfers*

	Mother	Daughter	Housekeeper
Monday	—	Lunch	—
Tuesday	—	Lunch	—
Wednesday	Lunch	Lunch	Lunch
Thursday	—	—	Dinner
Friday	—	—	Lunch
Saturday	—	—	Dinner
Sunday	—	Lunch	—

During that week the mother was invited to eat once at a relative's home and the daughter was invited four times by friends. In addition the domestic was invited out by friends to eat lunch (twice) and dinner (twice). All of these meals were paid by someone else which reduces the expenses of the household in regards to food consumption.

In the same segment of the Béké population we have interviewed another household to contrast with the previous, divorced, one to see if there are differences in the pattern of interhousehold transfers. This second household comprises a husband, a wife, three children, and a servant.

The family's meals out for one week are shown in Table 3.2. On Friday the entire household was invited to spend the day at a friend's house outside of Fort-de-France. The housekeeper came along to take care of the children. The husband estimated that, if taken at home, the meals would have cost the household about 250 francs.

TABLE 3.2   *Interhousehold Transfers*

	Husband	Wife	Three Children	Maid
Monday	—	—	—	—
Tuesday	—	—	—	—
Wednesday	—	—	—	—
Thursday	—	—	—	—
Friday	Lunch Dinner	Lunch Dinner	Lunch Dinner	Lunch Dinner
Saturday	—	—	—	Lunch Dinner
Sunday	—	—	—	Lunch Dinner

A companion case from Lower Sainte Thérèse shows similar features in interhousehold transfers among both groups. A lower-class couple took a loan for 6000 francs from the Bank of Paris to purchase a Renault 9. Also at the same time a friend in need got a loan for 200 francs from them. We also learn from this couple that they receive guests for dinner at least twice a month and they are invited to eat at a friend's or relative's home approximately twice a month.

The following example shows in different ways how interhousehold transfers are accomplished in some cases. In a two-bedroom rented house in Sainte Thérèse lives a family headed by a woman. She has been there for five years and pays 1250 francs per month. When she was 29 years old, she left her mother's house at Vauclin and came to look for employment in Fort-de-France. She lived with a man for a while, but after she became pregnant by another man, she left the house and moved back to Vauclin to live with her mother. The second man never lived with her but simply came to visit her and his son once in a while. She stopped seeing him when she moved back to Sainte Thérèse. In addition to her son she lives with two nieces, the daughters of her brother and of a sister who has died.

This example offers a very good view of interhousehold transfers and how the system functions from one generation to the next. Here one finds a case of a pregnant woman who reintegrated herself in her mother's household and later integrates her nieces into her own household. Such family solidarity has helped family members in various occasions to cope with the constraints of life and poverty transgenerationally.

MERGERS

Merger is often caused by poverty, and may indirectly be an important element in the reproduction of poverty. By merger I mean the process by which two different households coalesce in order to form a single household that is more stable under the present circumstances. All the members of one household or only some members may take part. The merger may be transitory or permanent. It is transitory when incoming members stay for a while in their newly found residence but soon move out. This was the case of urban dweller Josephine, who with her daughter returned to live with her mother after her husband divorced her. A year and a half later, she got a job and moved out with her daughter to a small house she rented.

A merger is said to be permanent when incoming members have no intention of leaving the household they join. This was the situation of an older couple who had come to live in Volga Plage with their married daughter. The daughter had invited them to join the household, since they were often sick; it was expected that they could help with babysitting.

In the neighbourhoods of Fort-de-France, when two households merge, it is likely that one household is in difficulty and the other stable. The one with problems joins the stable one and not vice-versa. I have not found any situation in which two households both in severe difficulties merge together.

Mergers are an especially significant form of interhousehold transfer. When they occur, one household is subsumed into another;

for the time being at least one member will have lost status as the head of a household. He or she is now living under the authority of another head. Roles are adjusted to meet the new social conditions. In such mergers not every member will participate; some will move to form new homes, just as in a firm not every person is incorporated into another pre-existing firm.

RISKS

The success of the family-household as a firm may depend on its ability to handle risks. No investment, whether in social, human, or physical capital, can be conceived of as risk-free. In the running of a household the head and the other members as well take risks that eventually will be useful or detrimental to the welfare of the household. In other words the risk factor can also be a source of the reproduction of poverty.

Taking risks is part of any enterprise; some are good and others bad, either in terms of means used or the results obtained. A good risk, long-term or short-term, yields good returns and a bad risk yields negative ones. Part of the decision-making process in the household is to evaluate risky behaviour and avoid risky situations. In the household, risks are taken in the light of the knowledge accumulated by all the members.

Probably the most potentially costly risk taken by residents of Volga Plage was to build their houses on state land. They did it in the hope that the state will not evict them, but also in awareness that their houses could be bulldozed by the state at any time. They regularly take the risk of participating in the *sousou* (a Martinican rotating credit association) in the hope there will be no default. Taking risks is part of the everyday life of the dwellers in the poor neighbourhoods of Fort-de-France.

BANKRUPTCY

Members of the family-household may learn various trades in order to prevent the unit from group bankruptcy. The notion of bankruptcy here refers to the collapse of the household as a viable economic unit. Various factors may lead to such a fate. Unemployment and underemployment may provoke a structural crisis or cyclical crisis in the operation of the household. When costs are greater than revenue or when too many unproductive members are added to the household, eventually the family will experience a crisis that may lead to its dissolution.

When bankruptcy threatens, there are several options to be considered. Absorption of the members into another household may be a solution to the crisis. However, dispersion is also common. Such scattered family members may be incorporated into several other households. It may also happen that only some members leave and are reabsorbed elsewhere or form a new unit. The end result, here in the case of the dissolution of the household and the reincorporation of members into another unit, is not very different from what happens to the firm that goes through a bankruptcy crisis.

Among the multitude of causes thay may lead to the dissolution of the household, unemployment and incorporation of new members seem to be especially significant. The reproduction of poverty occurs here in terms of the presence of extra household members who are not income providers but simply extra mouths to feed. However, household dissolution is not in itself a problem; it becomes a problem when the breadwinner takes his or her income away from the household that has come to rely on it.

SUBSIDIARIES

Another strategy by which the household may prevent the reproduction of poverty in its midst is the development of subsidiaries. Subsidiaries are legitimate extensions of a business venture or a household. Like the firm, the household may develop its own subsidiaries both domestic and overseas. Such a subsidiary may be thought of as an extension or branch of the household headquarters. It is formed for different reasons and may either strengthen or weaken the possibility for survival of both households. An informant from Sainte Thérèse explained how her family was affected by this strategy. 'My older daughter could not find employment here and we helped her financially to travel to Paris. We continued to send her some money during the first year. At that time, we had a good *boutique* that functioned well. She married her husband who was working at the Post Office in the seventh Arrondissement. My husband died three years ago and my daughter helps me financially. She wants me to come and live with them in Paris, but I prefer to stay here.'

Martinican migration to metropolitan France generally follows the same pattern. Members migrate in order to develop a branch of the household elsewhere. In the beginning of the process the migrants may receive financial aid, and this may continue even during the settlement period; but once established, the migrants are expected to send money back to the members of the family remaining in the island.

When problems arise in the household headquarters, the subsidiary is expected to advise or even to take control. For this reason the subsidiary households may finance the migration of other members, to alleviate the burden on the headquarters, but also to give others the opportunity to branch out. Over time, as the headquarters decline in importance, an overseas subsidiary may become the headquarters and the household of origin take a dependent position.

The headquarters household may go through an *expansion* process to strengthen its basis of support and operation, especially with a view to augmenting its overall revenue. It may also go through a *contraction* process to minimise its overall cost; this may be seen through the mergers where overhead costs tend to decrease.

FAMILY NAMES

Like a firm, the family-household may develop a good or bad name and may benefit from or be stigmatised by the reputation attaching to its members. Some firms are known by their image: the name tells it all – such as for example, IBM. One may choose to buy or not to buy from a firm solely on the basis of its reputation.

In a small island like Martinique it is easy to recognise the family-households that develop or inherit a good name or reputation, and just as easy to know those that do not. The household name may be associated with wealth, political power, generosity, goodness, brightness, and the like. Sometimes name may be a consideration in the choice of one's partner in marriage, in business, or for friendship. In Martinique to marry into the family of Aimé Césaire – the distinguished poet and mayor of Fort-de-France – is considered by many to be an honour, and is a definite plus for those with political ambitions.

To explore one more facet of the reproduction of poverty, let us address the hierarchy of households in Fort-de-France. People benefit from the good reputations of their family-households in the island, through access to influential people who can help them in case of need.

Those with well-regarded names find themselves in a social environment they can exploit to their own advantage. Insofar as a name may be a factor of upward mobility it is an advantage that the poor residents may not have.

CONCLUSION

The thrust of this chapter has been the argument that the family-household should be studied as a multiproduct firm to understand how its serves as a niche for the reproduction of poverty.[5] I do not propose that it is an exact counterpart of the typical firm; it is nonetheless a firm on its own merits.

The family-household can be seen as a multiproduct firm because of the diversity of its output and also because it is involved in the capitalist process of accumulation. It allows one to understand the dynamics of household life and the economic rationale behind the stratification and domination factors in the organisation of the family-household. It operates like any typical multiproduct firm, which indeed I think evolved from, and on the principle of, household organisation. In other words the historical origin of the firm is to be found in the organisation of the household.

The family-household is not an exact counterpart of the firm because it is, of course, a household first and a firm second. The ultimate goals of the firm and the family-household are in some ways different. The ultimate aim of the family-household is the welfare and happiness of the members, whereas in the case of the firm it is profit. The family-household does not put profit maximisation above the welfare of its members. One also notices that family-household decisions are not always taken with a monetary economic purpose. Sometimes taste preferences seem to prevail, as when members buy expensive clothes or go to an expensive restaurant. Neither does the family-household fire unproductive members in the way the firm does. That human and personal aspect distinguishes the family-household from the firm, but also distinguishes the content of interpersonal relations between both entities.

Reproduction of poverty sometimes is a correlative of the reproduction of wealth. If a household is able to reproduce its wealth through the exploitation of its employees, it may contribute to the reproduction of poverty in its midst. An example here is the household that hires a domestic servant at a low wage, exploiting her in the same way firms use and exploit illegal aliens.

However, to understand the basic mechanism of the reproduction of poverty in the slum and squatter settlements of Fort-de-France, one must not underestimate the external exploitation. The poor urban household sells its labour power for a price that is well below its value. The money is used partly to buy commodities priced higher than their worth. In the process the labourer is exploited twice and contributes unwillingly to the daily reproduction of poverty in his or her own family.

The family-household develops strategies to fight its battle against poverty. However, unemployment and the cultural practice of feeding extra mouths are negative factors that help reproduce poverty by making it very difficult to accumulate capital.

The study of the family-household as a multiproduct firm allows us to identify the causes of urban poverty and the mechanisms of its reproduction. It shifts our focus from the household to the typical firm. The causes of failure in the firm are the same as those behind the failure of the managerial operation of the household. They can be summarised into three major categories. First, the policies of the state may be an hindrance to the extent that they do not help family in need and do not create the conditions in which families prosper. Examples here are the inability or unwillingness of the state to intervene on behalf of the poor or to provide welfare benefits. Second, the poor may not succeed in overcoming their burden if external market conditions are not favourable, for example, if they are unable to find jobs. Third, the first two problems may be compounded if people lack managerial skills (take bad risks, make bad decisions, and so forth) in the operation of the household; and one may finally add plain 'bad luck', that is, a series of circumstances (illness, for example) that are beyond one's control.

The idea of the family-household as a multiproduct firm has also a number of practical implications. Two examples will suffice here. First, this methodological approach allows a better understanding of the household and of how to influence its course. A problem in one avenue of the life of the household may trigger a chain reaction that leads to poverty. Proper intervention in the form of a well-thought-out system will require a diagnosis, to identify the ultimate or first cause, and a therapy that consists in a proper intervention.

Second, if this analysis is correct, and I believe it to be so, even within a socialist or communist state the family-household will still be a capitalist enterprise because of the urge to accumulate capital for the preservation of the household and the urge of individual household members to improve their material standard of living. The household remains a centre of contradiction where state goals and policies contrast and clash with household goals. It seems likely that a certain level of repression or state control will be necessary to keep the family-household in line with state practices and objectives.

NOTES

1. There is now a large body of literature on the theory of the firm. To get a sense of issues raised in this literature, see Loon (1983), Laitinen (1980), and Williams (1978).
2. The notion of the household as a 'multiproduct firm' was first suggested by Margaret Reid (1974). However, to my knowledge, it was Simon Fass (1978) who made the first attempt at studying the household as a firm in a Ph.D. dissertation that he wrote on poor Haitian families in the capital city of Port-au-Prince.
3. In their book, *Mass, Class and Bureaucracy*, Bensman and Rosenberg (1963, p. 101) refer to the housewife as a 'general manager'. They further add that she 'achieves status as a major decision-maker' (1963, p. 101).
4. Fass's findings in Haiti can also be applied to the Martinican urban situation. He wrote that 'children are sometimes sent to fond relatives such as a childless sister, a widowed mother, or a lonely father to keep them company and help them out in their economic activities . . . . Given that women receive funds from men outside the sample population, we ought to expect that the reverse is true and that men in the sample draw part of their earnings away from their households to support others' (Fass, 1978, pp. 42, 147).
5. Earlier studies on the Martinican family have focused on the phenomenon of matrifocality, mating patterns, household composition and related issues (see Dubreuil, 1965; Horowitz, 1967; and Slater, 1977).

4 Domestic Workers

A phenomenon that is part of the urbanisation process in the Caribbean is the presence of domestic workers in middle and upper-class homes. In urban Martinique two historical facts have shaped contemporary domestic service: the colonial past, and the transformation of the island into a Department of France in 1946. The colonial period was the cultural mould in which workers and patrons created the symbolic content of their asymmetric relationships; with departmentalisation, social security laws defined a new social context and new modes of interaction.[1] By shifting the Martinican economy from its plantation base to one heavily subsidised by Paris, departmentalisation occasioned the incorporation into the market economy of individuals who by their position in the household were not wage earners.[2]

Since 1946, Martinique's employers have had to contend with the recognition by the state of the civil rights of domestic workers, who are protected by the law against such abuses as being fired without notice or subject to sexual exploitation. The new legislation also provides domestic workers with economic protection if they lose their jobs or become disabled. The new arrangement places the burden on the patrons of social security payments on behalf of their workers.

Nevertheless, in urban Martinican society paternalist relations and attitudes toward domestic workers continue to be a common denominator. Although the laws limit the opportunities for exploitation in terms of working hours and the conditions of the workplace, and introduce paid fringe benefits, such laws do not change people's attitudes or patterns of behaviour. Consequently a strictly legalistic appoach may not be sufficient to shed light on the social context of domestic life.

In this book I propose that urban poverty can best be understood through a careful analysis of the strategic institutions that breed and maintain inequality. The ecology of urban poverty is seen as comprising a network of institutions that cater to the needs of lower-class individuals. It is precisely in the study of the content, operation, and dynamics of these institutions that we will be able to see clearly the production and reproduction of poverty. Urban domestic work, because it is an institution that permits us to follow with some precision the production and reproduction of poverty, is the focus of this chapter.

The study of the family in the Caribbean has tended to focus on either husband or wife, the two 'integrated' members of the domestic unit.[3] The domestic worker provides another perspective from which to view the production and reproduction of poverty within the confines of the urban Martinican household. This fresh approach is important on three counts. First, it compels us to examine the impact of the domestic's presence on the everyday life of the household; second, it makes it possible to understand the fragility of the interstitial social position of the domestic; and third, it sheds light on the functioning of the domestic's own family.

TYPOLOGY OF DOMESTIC WORKERS

Domestic workers are exploited both individually and as a group. Their exploitation differs solely in degree, not in kind. Some receive a daily wage similar to that of other workers in the public and private sector, while others do not. In Martinique the domestic is almost always a woman. The extent of exploitation to which the domestic is subjected is related to her ability to overcome the burden of poverty in her own household and to the reproduction of poverty in that household.

To understand the phenomenon, we will begin with a typology of domestic workers. First, there are young women placed voluntarily or involuntarily in urban homes to provide the residents with such services as cooking, cleaning, and baby-sitting, and who in return are provided with shelter, food and clothing. For the most part they tend to be orphans or young persons whose parents are unable to take care of them. The testimony of several informants indicates that this form of domesticity is declining. Foster children from lower-class families who are placed in middle and upper-class homes – unless they are related consanguineously with the residents of the household – end up similarly serving as domestic workers.

Second, there are full-time adult workers, who are paid for their services. They are told beforehand the kind of work they are hired to do and what the working hours will be. They have complete freedom to organise their time after work and may refuse to perform certain types of labour. They receive a monthly salary and the patron pays social security on their behalf.

Third are part-time paid workers. These individuals are hired for shorter periods of work, for example, half days. They do not eat lunch at the patron's house. The same worker may be engaged in more than one household. One individual, for example, may spend three hours each in three different homes, or in a combination of work in private homes, private enterprise, and the public sector. Those who do ironing or baby-sitting fit into this category. Such domestics are not generalists, but rather specialise in the performing of specific types of labour.[4] Workers who are engaged in more than one job may have their social security paid by only one or by more than one employer.

In each situation described there are modes of relationship that can be understood in terms of the length of employment and intentions of both actors. It is likely that the domestic worker who has been working for the same family for several years will develop close ties with them. She has invested her time and made some commitment to be useful to that family. Both patrons and domestic workers go into the relationship with the good intention to work out their differences and to make each other happy. This is precisely the kind of commitment characteristic of the *gouvernante* or the *da*, but such arrangements are declining. Early this century the *da* was a full-time member of the household where she worked, ate, and slept. Victor Sévère (1931, p. 287), a former mayor of Fort-de-France, described the creole *das* who, instead of baby-sitting small children at home, took them to the Savane (a city park) where they could run and play at ease.

Often the relationship is less rewarding because one party is not forthcoming about her commitment. There are cases, for example, where the domestic worker takes a job on a temporary basis without informing the employer of her intention. Her level of commitment is very low, since she knows that she is not going to stay long. There is also the case of the family who hires a domestic worker only for a few weeks but make that person believe it will be a permanent job. The longer a domestic worker works in a home the more likely she will be integrated in that home.

RECRUITMENT

Recruitment, because it provides entry to the employer's household, is an indicator in the mechanism of the reproduction of poverty. To the extent that the employer knows the applicant, either as a distant relative or an acquaintance, there is a chance that the employer may threaten her financially and otherwise. To put it differently, those who are hired with no previous relationship with the owner of the house are more likely to be exploited and to be treated in a harsh manner. The relationship of the employer to the employee is one of a business nature.

The mode of recruitment of domestic workers tells us much about their integration in the family. Martinican families use five ways to recruit domestic workers in their homes. Some workers are found through a third party, a friend or acquaintance. One may ask a friend for help in looking for a worker. Sometimes one may be informed of the availability of a worker, or a worker may be referred to one's house. Commonly a family will steer an unneeded worker to another family; and if a worker quits her job, she may introduce a relative to the family to replace her.

Other workers offer their services from door to door. This is done frequently in Didier, a neighbourhood in which several Béké families still live, the descendants of French colonists. Getting hired in this way is a matter of presenting oneself at the proper time, when a family is looking for a worker.

Domestic workers and patrons increasingly use the columns of the newspapers *France-Antilles* and *Von Von* to announce, respectively, availability for work or positions in their homes. Usually those who seek employment in this manner tend to be well-educated; they could easily find work in another sector of the economy if jobs were available. During the month of July 1985, a large number of young women informed the people of their availability for domestic work by placing ads in *France-Antilles*. Among them, many had been trained as secretaries.

The 'Metro families', immigrants from metropolitan France, including civil workers and army personnel, most frequently use the formal institutions or such agencies as ANPE (Agence Nationale pour l'Emploi) to look for workers. If these families are newly-arrived immigrants, they will not have the contacts to do otherwise. Likewise, women who do not have any contact with this sector of the employer market find domestic jobs through a government agency such as ANPE. This is a last resort for experienced workers because there are more risks involved: neither party knows what to expect from the other.

The fifth mode of recruiting a worker is one with a long tradition. Some people visit the countryside in search of a domestic worker, having decided not to hire young women from the city because they may be more difficult to deal with. Such employers believe a rural woman is likely to be more modest, less demanding, and readier to show respect toward the family. She may be untrained, but she is perceived as being malleable.

DOMESTIC WORKER – FAMILY RELATIONSHIPS

The experience of the domestic must be seen *in situ*. Over time the domestic may become closer to the patron's family and more 'integrated' in her role. Accordingly the length or time spent in domestic work may have an influence on her own family. Although there exist in the metropolitan area of Fort-de-France some male domestic workers, our focus will be on female domestic workers in private homes. According to Horowitz (1967, p. 16) 'in 1961, more than 8,000 women, about 25 per cent of all women employed, were household workers'. The census of 1982 reports a total of 4934 domestic workers living and working in Fort-de-France, of whom 878 are males (gardeners) and 4056 females. It also shows that in the city 11 per cent of all working women were domestic workers, and 60 per cent of the female population were unemployed (Institut National de la Statistique, 1983, p. 104).[5]

The reproduction of poverty in the domestic's household depends a great deal on the reproduction of the relations of dominance and subservience in the employer's household. The inferior and interstitial position of the domestic in the employer's household is daily reproduced. How this is accomplished is discussed below.

The domestic servant's involvement with the family may vary from one member to another, depending on the structural position of the family member. The presence of the worker may be a source of both conflict and comfort. The presence of the domestic in a house provides for the family a sense of its self-worth. The wife's status is enhanced by the fact that another female does the work she would normally have to do.

In many cases the relations of the domestic with the husband and wife remain a benevolent form of paternalism. She is often reminded subtly that she is a lower-class member of the household. The kind of relationship the husband (or an older son) maintains with the domestic may define the contours of the relationships of the domestic with the rest of the family. The paternalist attitude develops most readily when the husband is not involved sexually and emotionally with the domestic worker.

The husband's sexual involvement with the domestic often creates a problem in the household. One can easily imagine the conflict that may emerge between the wife and the domestic. My informants tell of cases in which the domestic became pregnant and was obliged to leave the house. Sometimes the wife is unaware that the baby is her husband's. The problem is no longer as acute as before the departmentalisation of Martinique. Now an affair may go unnoticed because of the availability of birth control. If a worker becomes pregnant, this is likely to be intentional, because if paternity is proved (and this is often not too difficult) the child will have legal rights to his father's inheritance.

Sexual involvement of the domestic with an older son may be less dramatic for the well-being of the household. An informant in Terres-Sainville, a middle-class neighbourhood of Fort-de-France, said he would not advise his son to sleep with the domestic, but if he decided to do so would not blame him. In fact he would be in favour of it, provided it concerned only consenting adults. After all, he said, 'My boy needs that kind of experience'. However, if the woman were to become pregnant he would not recognise the child, because he thinks that 'it would be a shame to bring a lower-class person in the family'.

To avoid this problem, it is likely to be the wife who chooses the domestic worker. As a result, younger women have less chance of being selected by a younger couple. It is believed that when the husband shares in the selection process he may hire someone with the possibility of sexual advances in view.

The situation of the woman who refuses to sleep with the patron is extremely delicate. In fact any decision she makes is likely to cause problems. If she accepts, she finds herself competing with the wife for the same man. If she does not accept, she may be fired by either the husband or the wife. One informant told the story:

When I was a younger woman, I used to serve as a domestic in a mulatto family. The family was nice to me and there was a great trust between us. One day the patron asked to sleep with me. I did not say yes because I did not want to lose my job. I told him at some later time that I did not want to get involved with him. In the meantime, I told the wife who was a good friend about the proposition in the hope that she will ask the husband not to insist any further. I thought that will be the right strategy to save my job. His wife told him that she was aware of the incident. He became violent verbally and I was forced to leave the job. And I believe this has created a problem between the husband and the wife as well.

There are, however, cases in which a discreet relationship between the husband and the domestic did not create any marital uproar. One such was described by an older woman from Lower Sainte Thérèse:

> When I was working for Monsieur X he asked to sleep with me. We had an affair and his wife was not aware of that. He used to give me gifts and he thought that he was not well treated by his wife and I believed him. He would drive the wife to her work place and he would come back to sleep with me. This affair lasted several years and when I had my boyfriend I stopped playing with him. I believe that he is still living with his wife. We used to treat each other differently, depending on the presence or the absence of the wife. In the presence of the wife, I used to call him Monsieur. In the absence of the wife, he used to call me *doudou* or *chérie*.

Sometimes the relation can become so intense that the man may end up marrying his domestic worker. Probably the most spectacular case is that of a well-known politician of Sainte Thérèse, a lower-class neighbourhood in Fort-de-France, who had been with his worker for several years and had a couple of children by her. While his wife was sick the maid took care of her. When the wife died, he married the domestic worker who was already his mistress.

At other times the wife, unaware of the relationship between the husband and the domestic worker, may serve as an unwitting accomplice. This was the story of an informant who had a child by her employer:

> I was a domestic worker in a Béké home. The Béké had coerced me to have sexual relations a few times with him. His wife was not aware of our affair. I became pregnant and had a baby girl. I left the house when I became pregnant and told her that the child was from an old-time boyfriend. However, I continued to work for the family. My daughter used to come to the house with me. The Béké knew that the child was his and the wife had no idea whatsoever. My daughter knew that her father was a Béké. However, there were no relations between the children of the wife and my daughter. I must add that the wife of the Béké used to give me in secret some extra money to take care of the child.

It may also create an uncomfortable situation for the family when the older son is involved sexually with the worker. An informant tells us that the employer's son took advantage of my niece, who was a domestic worker in the household. She became pregnant and the parents of the boy were very unhappy because he lowered the reputation and the social class of the family. The parents of the boy did not want to take any responsibility in the affair. They felt ashamed not because their boy would sleep with a domestic but because he had a child by her. The parents of the girl were also ashamed of her. She was entrusted to that family and they were disappointed. Both families were unhappy, but for different reasons.

The girl was blamed by both sides.

The domestic of long standing may have such good relations with the family that she even serves as their adviser or counsellor when marital problems emerge. 'On several occasions', an informant says:

the wife was crying in her room and I went to console her. At other times, she would call me and asked for my advice when she was having problems with her husband. I remember once both were arguing in the living room and when I came in both started talking to me. She placed her head on my shoulder and was crying. As I was consoling her, I also gave her and her husband some good advice. They were young. They treated me like their mother and I treated them like my children.

Frequently the worker may intervene, instructing a child to obey his parents. She may be the best friend of the children when they are young.

The domestic worker is the link between her family and her patron's family. The intensity and form of the relationship depends on several variables. In the majority of cases, since the domestic works as a day labourer and returns home in the evening, the relationship may be a casual one. Since the domestic is not expected to take her children to work with her, the patron's family may not have an opportunity to meet the domestic's family. If the domestic has an affair with, or a child by, the patron, the relationship between the two families may become more intense. In some cases the patron actually maintains two different households. The domestic serves in the patron's house not only as a domestic but also as a mistress. The domestic's children may know who their father is, but are unable to relate to their half brothers and sisters as siblings.

Ordinarily it is in the organisation of the domestic's family that the influence of the patron's family may be felt the most. If the domestic has dependents, for example, and is the only paid worker in her own family, any financial difficulty encountered by the patron will have immediate consequences in the domestic's family. Any significant difficulty between the domestic and the patron will also have some immediate ramifications in her own family. For that matter the domestic's family can be influenced in several ways by the patron's family.

OLD AND NEW PATRONS VERSUS OLD AND NEW DOMESTICS

Although the exploitation of the domestic worker has remained constant in Martinican history, the social origins of the actors have changed over time. In the process the content of the relation of domination has also fluctuated, but the main result, that is, the production of inequality and the reproduction of poverty, has remained the same. The evolution of that practice is discussed below.

The evolution of the domestic worker's status in Martinique can be related to a series of factors, including the restructuring of the economy, protective laws, technological changes, and the attitudes of both patrons and domestics toward the job. This evolution is also registered in the common terms by which the domestic is referred to. In the era before departmentalisation, Martinicans referred to them as *da* (domestic worker), *bonne* (domestic) or *gouvernante* (live-in maid). Now Martinicans use *femme de ménage, gens de maison* or *femme de maison* (all translatable as housekeeper). This is understood to be a paid job, based on an informal contract sanctioned by law.

There has also been an evolution in the patron's needs, and in the kind of work requested from the domestic. This is partly related to technological change. For example, the domestic is no longer requested to handwash clothes, since the washing machine will do the same amount of work in a shorter period of time. Gas or electric stoves are less demanding than coal or wood-burning stoves. In the past, domestic workers worked for patrons who lived usually in their own private homes, with large families. Now the family of the patron tends to be small, and many live in apartments.

In historical terms, departmentalisation caused an occupational shift in the servant-employing Béké segment of Martinican society. Before 1946 local whites were mostly plantation owners, and each

Béké family had two or more workers. With departmentalisation many have shifted to industry or to the import/export sector of the economy. In the process of that change many have sold their large homes in Didier. According to the 1982 census those still living in Didier now employ no more than one worker, and occasionally a gardener.

As the number of workers in Béké families have become smaller over the last three decades, new employers have also emerged. Many are members of the new middle-class, individuals who have benefited from the expansion of the Martinican economy, or who lived abroad for a period of time. Many of these families, especially those with young children and a working wife, have hired domestic workers. These families tend to have tight budgets and to pay their domestics less, even if they show more understanding or sensitivity to the domestic worker's plight, than do the rich bourgeois families.[6]

The patrons domestics feel most comfortable with are the Métro families who, because of their education and European upbringing, hold liberal and democratic ideas and are less prejudiced toward their domestics.[7] The domestic may be invited to eat with them, for example, and the wife may ask the domestic to call her by her first name, thus reducing the distance between them.

There is thus a diversification of patrons (local whites, metropolitan whites, and local Martinicans) that in part reflects class differences between middle and upper-class patron families. Diversification is also seen among the domestics. One finds both rural and urban lower-class Martinican domestics, as well as immigrants from St Lucia, the Dominican Republic, and Haiti, among others.

While the older type of domestics tended to include persons with little formal education who could not compete well in the labour market for jobs other than domestic work, the new domestics are educated; they may have worked in another type of job (as a secretary or saleswoman, for example); they may, for instance, specialise in one form of domestic work (baby-sitting, cooking); and they may take the job on a temporary basis.[8] They are individuals who, under other circumstances, would not do domestic work, and who consider the job as a stopgap or stepping-stone. These young women dress in such a way as to convey to the employer that this is a job they accept by necessity, not by choice. They are victims of cyclical constrictions of the labour market.

Both old and new patrons share perceptions of the evolution of the status of the domestic. It seems to them that before departmentalisation the domestic was a faithful worker, and that now she does it primarily for the money and demands more benefits, such as better living quarters. Patron-domestic conflict is no longer a private matter to be resolved by the patron, but may now involve the courts.

ECOLOGICAL AND SOCIAL STRATIFICATION

The home is the place where the daily exploitation of the domestic worker is materialised. A household reproduces inequality and consequently poverty through the establishment of a spatiotemporal order and an order of command related to social status and to one's position in the unit.

A family home is usually ecologically zoned in terms of the use of each room and its social functions for family members. Where there are sleep-in maids, the house is further divided into family rooms and the domestic's room. The family rooms are strategically located in the house and better furnished, but the domestic room may be marginal to the rest of the house, near the back door, or in a separate unit in the yard. The space occupied by the domestic may also have a symbolic value different from that of the rest of the house.

There are many reasons why the domestic worker occupies a space marginal to the house. First, the family is allowed more privacy in its movements and in interacting with visitors. The domestic is also allowed to have a space of her own, separate from the family. One domestic said that she was very grateful to her patron for such privacy because she was able to invite her boyfriend for the night and receive her friends and parents. After work she can leave and return without disturbing the rest of the house. Another informant was told that if she wanted to sleep out, she could do so, provided that she came back in the morning to prepare breakfast for the children. The domestic's room within the house is a kind of foreign territory to the rest of the family. It is a space that the members of the family are not expected to use routinely, as they do other rooms.

The structure of apartment life does not always allow such spatial separation between workers and patrons. When the patron's family lives in an apartment, the worker may even use the same bathroom facilities as the rest of the family.

The domestic worker is situated in time with respect to her employers. She wakes up before the other members of the family to prepare breakfast for them. Her entire daily work schedule is constructed around other people's needs. Her own volition is subordinated so that she can be useful as a worker, someone always ready to receive orders and help others.

The separation is felt also in the area of verbal address. The domestic refers to the patron as Mr or Mrs, with their surnames, while the patrons call the domestic by her first name. The inequality of status is maintained in address. Both paternalism and condescendence are symbolically expressed when an idiom of kinship is used. It is a way of easing the tension that may develop in the relationship between the patron and the domestic. The use of kinship terms or affectionate words is often times nothing more than a mask for exploitation.

The separation of the family and the worker is operational in still other ways. The domestic worker does not eat at the same time or in the same room as the patron's family. She eats either before or after the rest of the family has completed its meal. Sometimes the worker places the food on the table and later eats the leftovers. The worker may not get anything if the family likes the food. An informant recalls: 'Once I served or placed everything on the dining table and they ate everything. I was obliged to go to the shop and get something for myself. I ended up eating two eggs and some bread, because I was too tired to cook for myself.'

WORK SCHEDULE AND SALARY

The salary is the objective factor that accounts for the exploitation of the domestic. Through her work and salary, the domestic is involved in the creation of surplus value that is used by the homeowner or employer. The surplus value is the money accumulated by the employer as he provides the domestic with a wage below the real value of her labour. This surplus value contributes to the daily reproduction of the social position of both actors in the household. Since the surplus value is value not given to the domestic, her status in the household is also reproduced on a daily basis. The reproduction of the homeowner as a dominant figure and the reproduction of the domestic as a dominated figure are made possible by the reproduction of asymmetric relations between both entities. The salary, work schedule, and misunderstandings about responsibility for social security are factors that add to the burden of the domestic worker and that help explain the daily reproduction of poverty in her household.

The work schedule of the domestic is a point of contention and conflict in the household.[9] Sometimes the work is not precisely defined, and the domestic is expected to do whatever comes up. When the work is well defined, extra labour is paid for. In the more traditional form of domestic work, the worker is called to do everything. Thus the domestic cooks the meals, washes the clothes, irons them, takes care of children, and so on. Nowadays time and the content of the work are more clearly defined. The domestic may be told that she is expected to work from 8.0 a.m. to 7.0 p.m. or, if it is a part-time job, the number of hours is indicated. The domestic may do whatever she wants with her time after she has completed her job in the household. There is also now a tendency towards more specialisation. A person may be hired, for example, to iron clothes once a week or to baby-sit a number of hours per day or days per week. In any case paid domestics are hired to work only from Monday through Friday or Saturday noon; they follow the work schedule of the private and public sector. Even live-in maids are given free time and are no longer expected to work all day and night as formerly.

It is no longer possible to fire a domestic without advance notice. As an informant from Didier put it: 'The entire administration would rise against you.' The work itself has found a new image, and has gained some legitimacy, so much so that even high school graduates look for such jobs. Now domestic workers have their social security paid by the employer, and are entitled to five weeks vacation per year.

It is not easy to generalise about the income of domestic workers because there are so many variables to be taken into consideration. The average salary is between 1000 francs ($117.65) and 1500 francs ($176.48) per month. In addition their social security contributions are paid by the employers. If they are full-time workers, they may also sleep and eat there. Domestic workers who do not have a large number of dependants sometimes are able to save money and thus achieve upward mobility.

Sometimes there are informal monetary arrangements made between employers and employees. The employer, instead of paying social security for the worker, may pay her in cash half the amount destined for social security. Both parties feel they win something in this case – the employer pays less, and the employee gets more cash. The woman who enters such an agreement may already have been covered by her husband's social security. In any case the state is the loser, and the patron is the winner since he pays less.

The salary scale depends on the kind of services rendered. It is mostly in upper-class families that one finds full-time general domestic workers. In middle-class homes, specialists tend to work on a part-time basis. Some are hired as cooks and others as gardeners. The income of the domestic worker who is provided with housing and food is greater than the amount she is paid.

The legalisation of domestic work, while it has given state protection to workers engaged in this form of labour, has also created some confusion. The type of benefits the domestic workers are entitled to by law are not always clear to them. However, some use those protections to their own advantages. The following three cases illustrate this.

Case 1

A disabled young woman who had been receiving a monthly cheque of 2500 francs ($294.12) for *allocation adulte handicapée* decided to get a job. However, she did not intend to ask for any social security benefits because she thought that she was going to lose her monthly cheque from the state. She did find a domestic job and the patron happily agreed not to pay social security on her behalf. She worked part-time in the mornings. Neither she nor her patron contributed to her social security. Consequently she had no protection in case of an accident.

In this case the patron was able to keep for himself the money that by law he was supposed to deposit for the worker's benefit. This enlarges for the employer the surplus value created by the work of the domestic worker. Actually the domestic had misunderstood the terms of the law. She was entitled to work part-time, have her social security paid on her behalf, and still keep her allocation because of her disability. She thought that she was using the system to her own advantage, but in fact she was not.

Case 2

Another domestic worker worked for five days a week for two different employers: two days in one home and three days in the second. The owner of the second home left the island and returned to Paris. The worker made a request for *allocation familiale* or unemployment benefits. As Slater (1977, p. 97) notes, 'The allocation is a method of furnishing family assistance on a double basis: the number of children in a family and the number of days that one member of the family has worked for wages.' She was granted an allocation of 1000 francs ($117.65) per month. With her previous two jobs she made 1200 francs per month, from which she had to subtract 160 francs for transportation. Actually she made more money now than before and had no incentive to look for a second job.

This arrangement worked for both the domestic worker and the patron. Since she worked for only two days a week the domestic was more relaxed, spent more time at work, and did not ask for any salary increase. In order not to lose her *allocation familiale* she continued to work two days a week.

Case 3

This was the situation of a young woman who worked as a part-time domestic and lived with her parents. She had a daughter, not legally recognised by the father because the mother did not want to marry him. Because of her status and that of the child she received a monthly allocation for single parents of 900 francs ($105.89), for orphans of 250 francs ($29.42), and an additional familial allocation of 300 francs ($35.30). She was also able to have part of her social security paid by her employer in addition to receiving a monthly cheque from him. In this situation the domestic worker has clearly been able to take advantage of the system.

A SOURCE OF INFORMATION AND AN INTERMEDIARY

The worker serves as a source of information and an intermediary between the employer and the rest of the neighbourhood. That is an extension of the function of the domestic, in that it allows the employer to maintain his superior position by keeping a certain distance *vis-à-vis* the rest of the community. It is also a function that confirms to the worker her own inferiority *vis-à-vis* her employer.

The domestic is, for the rest of the neighbourhood, a source of information concerning the day-to-day activities of the family. This is particularly the case of the domestic who works for a Béké or Métro family which does not deal on a personal level with the neighbours. Any information that one might gather on such families is likely to be provided by the domestic. Labetan (1982, p. 85) provides an example of such a case in the thirties in Terres-Sainville. He reports that the worker Eulalie who worked in a French government offical house had her own network of friends in the neighbourhood, among them the clerk at the pharmacy with whom she talked and gossiped whenever she came to buy China tea for her employers.

The worker is also a kind of unofficial intermediary between the family and the neighbours. If the family is made up of 'important' people, one may even need the help of the domestic to see them. The domestic may make the decision concerning whether or not to let someone into the house. Because she answers the telephone, she controls access to her boss. She also plays the intermediary role whenever she is sent as a messenger by the family to see or carry things to other people.

In the vocabulary of the firm the domestic worker can rightly be considered a 'public relations' person. She has a good understanding of what goes on in the household, passes the information to others and informs the family of outsiders' reactions. She knows the whereabouts of every family member, since she is the one who spends her days in the house, and she communicates this information to individual family members. She may pick up the information from a family member and pass it on to another. As a public relations person, she may even exaggerate things in order to enhance her own status in the eyes of others.

INSULTS

Insults are one means used by the employer to make the domestic aware of her inferior position in the household. They are a way of psychologically harassing and terrorising the domestic. As mechanisms of social control, they are factors that contribute in the short range to the reproduction of worker status and consequently of poverty in her household.

The domestic worker occasionally falls victim to the temperamental outbursts of the family. Condescending attitudes are revealed and a basic lack of trust emerges. Many domestics interviewed for this book complained that patrons have called them thieves. Whenever something is missing in the house, the domestic is the one blamed. Often the object was not lost but simply misplaced by a family member. Seldom will the family make its apologies to the domestic.

Another area of complaint is the amount of food provided to the domestic. Even in the affluent Béké families, they are not always given enough food to eat. Portions are controlled, and the domestics are often told that they eat too much.

CONCLUSION

On the basis of the data presented in this chapter the following observations can be offered. The dometic worker participates in her own exploitation, in a sense, by accepting to work in an inferior position in someone else's household, but it is likely that her decision is conditioned by her inability to find a better job in another sector of the economy. There are forms of labour that place people in a position of inferiority and also make them aware of their status. Domestic servitude is one such form.

The presence of the domestic in the family turns the unit into an arena in which class and class consciousness is experienced, and exploitation practised. The macrosystem of capitalist exploitation finds its micro-expression in the domestic unit. Class relations are mediated by the system of exchanges whereby services are rendered in exchange for food, shelter, and salary. The domestic occupies an interstitial zone between two families. In the patron's family she is both an insider and an outsider. She is an outsider in that she is not a blood relative; she was not born in that family but was incorporated afterward; but she is also an insider in that she plays a key role in nurturing and feeding the family. Furthermore, although she is an insider in her own family, she carries with her the experience acquired in her employers' household, experience that has its impact on her role in her own family.

Domestic work reduces the rate of urban unemployment and the pressure on the state to provide jobs to its people. Smith (1973, p. 192) has found that, in Peru, 'domestic service operates as an effective mechanism by which the national capital of Lima is able to accommodate at least a part of the flood of migrants to the city from the provincial regions of the country'. Domestic servitude takes an entire segment of the population out of the competition for jobs in the public sector and places them as workers in private homes. As Jelin (1977, p. 135) writes, 'The performance of domestic productive activities in urban areas is one adaptation of the low income family to the low wages earned by the gainfully employed members of the household.' It is in fact through this channel that some of the domestics have been acculturated to city life. Domestic servitude, however, is for some as a stepping-stone to upward mobility. There have been several cases in which the domestic was able to save some money to pay for the schooling of her children or even to buy a house. Domestic work is also used by some to exploit the system, as, for example, when a woman decides to work for a few months in order to be eligible for unemployment benefits. The number of these is small.

Domestic servitude, by allowing a wife to move to the arena of non-domestic work, contributes in important ways to the earning power of the employer's household. Her professional status may be enhanced as well as her money-making ability. Hiring a domestic liberates her from housework; but at the same time, she may continue to look on household work as domestic's work. Because the hiring of a worker places the male outside the arena of housework, rather than solicits his taking a share of those responsibilities, it helps perpetuate the myth that household work is women's work. Servitude therefore is and must be seen as a form of gender exploitation. It contributes to the production and reproduction of inequality.

For the majority of the workers, especially those with dependants, domestic work keeps them at a very basic level of survival. Few make enough money to save. Their monthly salary is entirely spent in taking care of their subsistence needs. They do not learn skills that could make them competitive in the open job market. As the years go by, they have fewer alternatives, other than to work full-time as domestics in a single home, or to do domestic work in more than one home. However one looks at the situation of the domestics, one sees them caught in a job structure that reproduces poverty.

Domestic service reflects a lack of employment for unskilled labourers in the larger society. Domestic servitude is a consequence and not the source of a problem that lies elsewhere. Servitude is simply one solution – and not the best one – to the problem of poverty.

Domestic service reproduces poverty in a number of ways. It reproduces the wage hierarchy in which only a portion of labour is remunerated. The patron keeps the surplus value of the domestic's labour. This arrangement maintains the domestic in a state of subsistence, and is a form of socially tolerated exploitation.

The organisation of the household space is a reflection of the total class and ethnic division of territorial space. It is also a reflection of the asymmetry of social relations; spatial domination is manifested in the room assignments and the symbolic order of the house. The socially inferior position of the domestic is spatially confirmed.

It is probably in the psychological and attitudinal domain that domestic work can best be seen as reproducing poverty. Here the worker is made to feel less worthy than the other members of the house simply because of the kind of work she does. This kind of work environment may lead to an ambiguous dependence on the patron, who thus defines the content of his or her asymmetric relationships with the domestic.

Finally it is important to make a distinction between the day-to-day reproduction of poverty and its transgenerational reproduction.

Domestic service fits more into the former category than the latter, at least in urban Martinique, because of the determination and sacrifices made by many of the workers so that their children will not have to experience similar hardships. Some succeed, but others do not.

NOTES

1.   On the departmentalisation question, see the very useful book by Sable (1955).
2.   One essay by Benoist (1968) and another by Petitjean-Roget (1983, 1852–71) place in its ecological context the evolution of the economy of Martinique.
3.   The literature on kinship and family organisation in the English-speaking islands is reviewed by Smith (1963), and in Haiti by Laguerre (1978). On the lower-class families in Martinique, see Slater (1977), Horowitz (1967), and Dubreuil (1965). On family organisation among the Béké segment of Martinican society, see Kovats-Beaudoux (1969).
4.   For example, while the general worker is called on to do everything, the specialist is asked either to cook, baby-sit, iron, clean the house, or take care of the garden. Individual domestics may be hired for each of these tasks. See also Duarte (1976: p. 92).
5.   The situation here is not too different from that of domestic workers in the Dominican Republic. Duarte (1976, p. 86) has found that in 1970 there were 31 115 female domestic workers in Santo Domingo, accounting for 12 per cent of the population of women in the labour force.
6.   Similarly Duarte (1976, p. 95) has found that in Santo Domingo middle-class families are more flexible in regard to their domestics, and sometimes even provide them with the opportunity to learn a trade or to attend school.
7.   In Malaysia domestic workers show a similar preference for European employers, and for similar reasons (see Armstrong, 1985).
8.   The status of domestic workers in secondary cities of the Caribbean has evolved more slowly than that of the domestics in the capitals. For example, a study of domestic workers in Santiago de los Caballeros, Dominican Republic, found that the majority were live-in maids who made in 1968 an average of 15 pesos per month (Lanz, 1969, pp. 197–207).
9.   For comparative material on domestic workers in Haiti, France, Ecuador, and the United States, see Rollins (1985), Martin-Fugier (1979), Katzman (1978), Salmon (1901), Taylor (1976), Nett (1966), Scott (1939), and Vernet (1935).

5 The Grocery Store as an Exploitative Niche

The *boutique* in Volga Plage or in Sainte Thérèse is a microcapitalist venture in a poverty ecosphere. This local economic institution shows the flexibility of the capitalist system, which operates and carves a niche for itself at the very bottom of Martinican society. In fact the *boutique* represents in Fort-de-France one of the tentacles of the capitalist state and is an extension at the local level of the major national economic institutions. The study of this kind of venture forces us to give particular consideration to the 'processes and institutions of social reproduction which stand behind and support the circuits of capital' (Dickinson and Russell, 1986, p. 2).

From a structural standpoint the *boutique* provides a niche – and is either coincidentally or as a direct result a dumping ground for a ready-made clientele of poor persons. It is the means by which national economic institutions can exploit the local people. It allows a local middleman the opportunity to link the economic and political centre to the periphery. Furthermore it is adapted to the needs of the people because it sells products on a microretail basis, and provides credit to the poor daily and routinely, and because its proximity to the residences of the neighbourhood makes it a convenient place to shop. One must also add that it contributes to the transfer of capital from the neighbourhoods to the economic élite.

In other words the *boutique* is one of the points of articulation of the neighbourhood with the national economic centre, since on the one hand it provides goods to the poor residents that they may not have access to elsewhere on a credit basis, and on the other hand it provides the wholesalers with an outlet for defective merchandise that they might not be able to sell elsewhere.

The contribution of the *boutique* to the reproduction of poverty is seen in the way it interjects itself as a strategic variable in the organisation of neighbourhood life. In other words in the management of the households, near a *boutique*, poor people take into consideration the daily foods they can acquire on credit from the *boutique*. The concern here is on the exploitation and the daily reproduction of poverty rather than on a transfer between generations.

FROM PLANTATION TO URBAN NEIGHBOURHOOD INSTITUTIONS

The history of the boutique is that of its intermediary role between the dominated and dominant sectors of Martinican society from the era of slavery to the present. Formerly it contributed to the reproduction of poverty to the extent that it was a mechanism for the exploitation of the poor through unequal exchange, and during the postemancipation era provided politicians with a base of operation to take political advantage of the inhabitants. To understand the role of the grocery shop in the slums of Fort-de-France one must turn the clock back to the colonial era. The cultural patterns in which patrons and clients organised their interaction took shape during this period. Some of the functions of the *boutique*, as it began then to be called, date back to the colonial era.

According to my informants the *boutique* on the plantation was the place where the most important economic transactions took place. In some cases it belonged to an overseer who ran it as an extra source of income. Sometimes it was simply a company store, operated by an overseer or manager. It was one link between the slaves and the outside world. However, it was after emancipation, in 1848, that the ties of patron-client relationships became strongest. Those who worked for a planter family received their salaries at the end of the week, at which time they congregated at the *boutique* to drink and pay off their credit.[1] The *boutique* was a meeting place where people came to socialise with others, indulged in plantation gossip, and sought advice for their family. As a consequence it strengthened plantation brotherhood and solidarity.

Each individual buyer had a credit line, represented by a notebook in which the item bought and its price were registered as well as the date. On Saturday the credit extended during the week was repaid with a portion of the money received from the planter. As most of the plantation workers could not read or write French, they were asked to put a circle or an X in the notebook where the items were listed. Often the owner did it himself.

During the postemancipation era, the *boutique* in the villages and cities of Martinique continued to play a similar role as both a business centre and a place where people congregated. It took on a further dimension, too, in becoming a political centre. That had been a nascent role on the plantation, which grew to its full potential in urban areas. People came to the urban *boutique* to exchange political opinions, to get information about political matters, and to develop political strategies. Individual candidates for elective offices held political meetings at the neighbourhood *boutique* and used it as a distribution centre for political pamphlets. The owner became a local middleman, passing bribes to prospective voters on behalf of the politicos. One informant recalled that politicians provided free rum and shoes to the *boutiquier* to give to specified individuals who gave them out in exchange for votes on behalf of their candidates on election day.

In a population of illiterates the shopowner was the only one who could write a *laisser passer* giving one permission to move cattle from one part of the island to another. He also helped people to write letters and read to them the letters they received. Many different kinds of transaction took place at the *boutique*. There the police collected information about the life of the people and hunted out the younger men for *service militaire*. The owner could provide this type of information to the police because he knew where his customers lived, and how: parents sent children to the store and the owner learned many details about their families. In addition to his economic role he also served as a link between the political centre and the periphery.

THE SITE

The site enters into the explanation of the reproduction of poverty through its structural position in the system. Although the *boutique* is located geographically in the slum, it occupies a structural position between the commercial élite and the slum dwellers. The site may enhance the ability of the *boutique* to exploit the people.[2] There are two ways to establish a *boutique* in the *quartier*. Sometimes the site is selected in advance with a view to locating strategically in the neighbourhood, offering easy access to the people. Such a *boutique* is then physically a separate structure.

Sometimes the choice of the site of the *boutique* is not planned in advance. Someone with a house may decide to use the front room, or the first floor if it is a two-storey house, as a *boutique*. The house serves then two functions: residence and business.

The site selected is a function of the density of the population. A *boutique* in an overcrowded area is likely to do better than in a place where there are few people. Selection in also a function of the needs of the population, which will have an effect on the choice of goods to be sold: they will naturally be those items that are demanded by the surrounding population.

The *boutique* occupies a central place in the slum. In Lower Sainte Thérèse slum the *boutique* always faces the main street, and behind it is the alley where residents have their houses or apartments. Each *boutique* serves a particular alley, and there is a constant movement of people between the *boutique* and houses in the same alley. Neighbours do not need to get dressed up to go there; the location makes it very practical for them.

THE NAME OF THE BOUTIQUE

The name of the *boutique* is its identity. It locates in time and space one important mechanism of the daily exploitation of the population and consequently in the reproduction of poverty in the neighbourhood. The *boutique* may or may not have a formally chosen name, but the people tend anyway to refer to it by the name of the owner – not the surname, but rather a nickname or one chosen to express the ethnic identity of the owner. The people in Sainte Thérèse might say, for example, 'Kay Fofo', (Fofo's shop) 'Kay Nonotte', or 'Kay Roro'. Ethnic identity is expressed in 'Moin Ka allé Kay Chinouaa' (I am going to the Chinese shop); sometimes the entire name of the owner is used, as, for example, in 'Kay Jean Alphonse' (Jean Alphonse's shop). For the slum dwellers, what is important is not the name of the shop but the name or ethnic identity of the owner.

THE CONTENT OF THE BOUTIQUE

The *boutiques* are for the most part small business units. They are small in terms of the space they occupy, the volume of merchandise they sell, and the amount of profit made by the owner. The neighbourhood *boutiques* do not specialise in the sale of any particular item; they are generalist ventures.

The *boutiques* sell goods in two broad categories: comestible and non-comestible. Among the comestible items are sugar, bread, butter, spices, and so on; and the non-comestible category comprises things such as notebooks, pencils, and other small items in daily use.

The internal and symbolic order of the *boutique* partly reflects the personality of the owner, the availability of space, and the law of supply and demand. The items that are in constant demand are placed closer to the counter, where the salesperson has easy access to them. The other products are exhibited further away from the counter. Food items are separated from non-comestibles.

The content of the *boutique* reflects to a high degree the dependence of the grocery store owner on the wholesalers and the dependence of the neighbourhood on the store owner. These dependency links reduce the likelihood that the neighbourhood will have easy access to so-called upper-class goods. Instead the *boutique* caters to the monetary capability of the residents and, indirectly, it reinforces the image of poverty among them. The relationship between monetary capability of the residents and the goods that are made available to them is part of the process that reproduces on the one hand the means of production, that is, the reproduction of wealth, and on the other hand contributes to the reproduction of exploitation, that is, the reproduction of poverty.

ADVERTISEMENT

Shop owners have developed their own ways to advertise their merchandise. They may simply place a product in a strategic location on the shelves so that the incoming buyers can see it. They may go one step further, by informing the clientele about the qualities of a specific item, especially when someone asks them for advice. Perhaps one of the most common strategies by which the shop owner advertises products is to use children as messengers. For example, it is customary for a grocery store owner to say to a child '*Va dire à ta mère qu'on a de la morue*' (go and say to your mother that the salt cod fish has arrived). This message will remind the woman both that she can buy the item and that she does not have to pay immediately.

Advertisement is used to entice people to buy so that the national and local structure of exploitation can be maintained. Advertisement is simply another of the links that bind the oppressors to the oppressed and that reinforces the process of reproduction of poverty at the household level.

THE CLIENTELE

The clients are those individuals who through the regular purchase of goods in the *boutique* participate in their own exploitation and contribute unwillingly to the reproduction of poverty in their respective households. There are three basic types of clients. In the first category one may place the permanent residents, who own or rent a house in the neighbourhood. These are the daily shoppers who support the *boutique* and who in return may have a credit line with the owner. The *boutique* developed to meet the needs of this permanent resident population.

The second category comprises the transient clients. These are individuals who live in another neighbourhood but who may stop once in a while to buy something here. The owner does not know them and may never see them again after one chance interaction. They are the outsiders who also support the *boutique*.

The third category includes individuals who live in the neighbourhood and who normally do business with one *boutique* in proximity to their residences. If this *boutique* does not have at the moment the goods they need, the clients will look for them in another *boutique*. This behaviour shows that a *boutique* does not maintain a permanent monopoly of the clients who live near its location.

PRICING

It is basically through the pricing phenomenon that the dweller is exploited by the *boutique*. The items are sold at a price much higher than they are worth. The price includes the profit to be made by the wholesaler and the retailer. Overpricing is an important element in the reproduction of poverty in the households of the poor neighbourhood. The price of the items in the grocery shop depends on a number of factors worth mentioning here: the wholesale price is regulated by the Chamber of Commerce, and the retailer is allowed to make a profit of no more than 30 per cent for each item in a transaction with clients. This is the law, but actually the profit may be greater. The retailer may price the item to bring a profit in the range of 1 to 30 per cent. Quantity is one of the determining variables in pricing. However, there is room for manoeuvre, because the Chamber of Commerce does not fix the price for small items or for packaged items that can be broken down into smaller units. For example, a retailer bought twenty envelopes from a wholesaler for 13 francs 50. She resells each envelope for 1 franc and gets 20 francs. Here she makes a profit of 6 francs 50. It is customary in her store for a client to buy one envelope at a time, not a pack.

It is worthwhile to give another example of the profit that can be made by the retailer. When purchased directly from a wholesaler, a pack of cigarettes costs 6 francs and contains twenty cigarettes. If a retailer resells it as a pack at 6 francs 10, he makes a profit of only 10 cents. When he sells them at retail, he prices each cigarette at 50 cents. This way he resells the content of the pack for 10 francs. In the retail he makes a total benefit of 4 francs. This simply means that a pack of cigarettes that the poor urban dweller can buy for 6 francs or for 6 francs 50, he or she ends up paying 10 francs for.

Two more factors that may influence the price of an item: the location of the store and whether or not it is owned by the proprietor. When the shop owner has to pay rent, he prices his items so that the cost will be picked up by the clients. The location may influence the price if there are losses due to stealing.

A great demand for an item may induce the owner to raise the price so as to enlarge his margin of profit. There are also different prices for regular clients and for visitors. The latter are asked to pay more for the same item. To verify this practice, I asked an informant to buy a bottle of Coca-Cola in his neighbourhood and at two other locations. In his neighbourhood he paid 6 francs 50 and in the two other places he bought the item for respectively 7 francs 50 and 8 francs.

Although there are several *boutiques* along the Maurice Bishop Avenue in Sainte Thérèse, competition among the owners does not seem to influence the way each one prices his or her items. Each *boutique* has a ready-made clientele, the people who live in the alleys behind the shop. For ordinary items, proximity is more important than shopping elsewhere for bargains.

The retailer is not the big profit maker. In fact he may earn barely enough to live by. It was calculated that the *boutique* buys close to 4500 francs worth of merchandise per week and that in an ordinary day in the slum the retailer may make as profit anything between 100 and 150 francs. A good portion of this profit is consumed daily if the owner does not have any other job; the money may be spent to buy food and sustain the family.

Accounting or bookkeeping in the *boutique* is not sophisticated. Most stores do not use an adding machine. Calculations are done mentally or written out by hand on separate pieces of paper.

THE TRANSACTION ITSELF

The transaction gives a human dimension to the process of

exploitation. It tells us that exploitation is not carried out solely by strangers who do not know their victims and are unknown to them. In fact, when one is exploited by or exploits acquaintances, one becomes less conscious of the exploitation; but the consequence is the same, in both contexts. It leads to the reproduction of poverty in the household of the victim.

The *boutique* is not a self-service store. The customer must request the items one after the other. Moreover the store owner may have to weigh on a scale and decide on the price before giving the item to the client. The transaction takes place at the counter, where the item is placed, and the client either pays or returns the credit notebook so that the purchase can be registered.

Most of the residents of the slum and the squatter settlement do not stock large quantities of food at home, but rather buy for a day's consumption or even from meal to meal. This pattern requires the people to return constantly to the store to buy ingredients needed for the next meal.

DRINKING SHOP

The shop also plays the role of bar or liquor store. Sometimes there is a drinking room attached to the grocery store. A person can buy the drink in the store and return to the attendant room to sit down. The alcohol sold is bought by the owner wholesale. Sometimes it is contraband liquor, that is, alcohol bought at a cheap price from a docker who has stolen it from a vessel or simply brought to the country illegally from another island.

The drinking crew is often composed of the same people, who know one another. Sometimes one pays for a friend or simply shares a glass. Not everyone remains in the room while drinking; some prefer to buy liquor to drink at home or simply to drink it while standing in front of the store or walking in the streets.

The room is not strictly speaking reserved for those who consume alcohol. In fact many come there in search of company. It is a place to relax, especially in the early afternoon during the summer, when it is terribly hot outside. The drinkers themselves may provide either bad or good company to the grocery store owner. To the extent that drinking takes people away from active labour and is a waste of their money, it must be considered an additional factor in the reproduction of poverty in the slum dweller's household.

CREDIT

One of the reasons why the *boutique* is so popular in the neighbourhood is because the people enjoy the credit given to them by the owner. That credit helps both the client and the owner. It makes two individuals known to each other, and as a consequence a relation of trust develops between them.

The period for which the credit is given may vary from one day (in which case the person is asked to repay the following day) to a week or a month. The time allowed depends on the personal relationship of the client and the shop owner and the source of income of the client.

Each client with a credit line maintains a notebook in which the item, the price, and the date of the transaction are written. The name of the client appears on the notebook. The shop owner also keeps a notebook to keep track of his or her debtors.

Bookkeeping is sometimes a problem. It becomes a problem especially when items sold or paid for are not recorded in both notebooks. Sometimes one member of the family may use another member's notebook without their approval or knowledge of the transaction. The person named on the notebook is responsible for all transactions recorded in it.

The amount of credit given to someone depends on that person's salary and social status in the community, things of which the shop owner is certainly aware. For this reason some individuals are required to repay by the end of the week, whereas others may wait until the end of the month, and some may add new purchases to their credit line while others cannot.

The credit transaction may produce a net gain or net loss for the shop owner. Clients may not be able to repay on time; others default while still others may move to a different neighbourhood where the shop owner is not in a position to trace them immediately.

Giving or accepting a credit line is a form of economic transaction. The buyer speculates on the possibility that the owner may forget to register the item in his notebook or may register it for a lesser amount of money. Both of these things happen in fact; but the owner also speculates on the possibility that the person may default, for various reasons. As the owner has a mark-up sometimes as high as 30 per cent on some items, default may not necessarily lead the business into bankruptcy.

Advancing a credit line to an individual buyer has three different rationales. One is to help the person who cannot pay immediately, which may be the most important reason from the buyer's point of view. The second is to give the buyer an incentive to purchase more than he or she needs. The buyer with a credit line usually buys more. This feature of credit explains how the slum dweller may become an active participant in his own exploitation and in the daily reproduction of poverty in his household. The third rationale is to keep the *boutique* in the process of renewing its stock and attracting the same and new clients. For example, there are perishable items such as bread that the owner may want to dispose of by the end of the day. He is able to sell them because of the credit he offers to the slum dwellers.

Abuses sometimes creep into the system. Individuals who are given an opportunity to purchase items on credit do not always repay their debt on time. In such a case the client may avoid meeting the store owner for a while because he or she owes money. This form of desertion leads to hard feelings, even to fights.

PURCHASE AND RENEWAL OF THE STOCK

Purchasing is the operation that allows the shop owner to renew his stock and make goods available to clients, and the wholesaler to sell his products. It is an important node in the mechanism of exploitation of the neighbourhood. To maintain its shop the *boutiquier* buys goods from wholesalers, on a routine basis, perhaps when the wholesalers' trucks stop by the shop.[3] The owner may or may not buy from the wholesalers' trucks, but in any case the goods are available if he decides to purchase them. The decision is based on what remains in stock. Sometimes an order is made by telephone and delivered by truck once a week.

Other shop owners prefer to go to the wholesaler's outlet or warehouse themselves. They are able to select what they need and receive a price reduction on their purchases. There is a kind of contract between the wholesaler and the retailer because the wholesaler uses the retailer for the distribution of his goods.

THE BANKING ROLE OF THE BOUTIQUE

On a Sunday in July 1985, I positioned myself to count for one hour the people who came to one of the *boutiques* in Sainte Thérèse. Fifty-six individuals came in between 12.0 a.m. and 1.0 p.m., comprising a total of eleven adult women, nine adult men, thirteen girls, thirteen boys, and ten small children who accompanied their mothers to the *boutique*. Most of the men came to buy cigarettes and beverages that they consumed in front of the *boutique*. Merchandise for household consumption was purchased mostly by adult women and their daughters and sons.

Because the credit notebook is not necessarily taken care of solely by the adult owner, but may be used by anybody in the household, misunderstandings arise from time to time between the client and the store owner. The purchase of one member of the family may be entered into the notebook of another. In the same household the mother and a working daughter may have different notebooks. Another source of confusion is that a patron may charge a messenger for an item purchased on behalf of another client. Although the messenger may inform the patron about the nature and terms of the transaction, the patron may inadvertently register the credit under the messenger's name.

Like any bank the *boutique* provides a 'credit line' to its customers; but more than that, the *boutique* provides an exchange service. During the hour of my observation, I noted some routine ways in which the *boutique* acted as a bank; three individuals requested change from the owner. Two came with a 50 franc bill; they needed small bills, probably to have exact change for their bus fares. The third needed to repay the loan from a neighbour. The *boutique* provides these services to attract clients to its retail operation, to accumulate paper money for the purchase of new stocks, and to get rid of unneeded small currency.

THE BOUTIQUE AS A FAMILY ENTERPRISE

Running the *boutique* is a strategy used by the family to overcome the burden of poverty. The *boutique*, which operates every day from 7.0 a.m. to 5.30 p.m., is by definition a family enterprise. It is owned by a family and the employees are all family members. Each *boutique* has its own history. It is worthwhile to analyse the formation and evolution of one of them, a *boutique* located in Volga Plage. This operation started after a young couple had moved to their new house. Even while they were building the house with the help of neighbours, they had the possibility of the business in mind.

The house has two storeys. The family lives upstairs and organises a *boutique* on the ground floor. Actually they began selling products before the house was completed, following the custom in Volga Plage of living in a house still under construction. Both the salary of the husband and the earnings from the *boutique* were used to complete the house.

The couple started the *boutique* with a small capital they had accumulated as personal savings. They enlarged their holdings according to the clients' demands. In fact the development of the *boutique* was due to the accumulation of capital, the completion of the house, and the growing size of the clientele.

However, the *boutique* could not have grown without the participation of various members of the family. For example, the wife is in charge of the operation, but she is helped by a daughter who replaces her when she is unavailable. A son also helps from time to time to pick up merchandise from the wholesaler.

Since it is a family enterprise, the shop is sustained by capital from the working members of the household. Although the husband and the wife are chiefly responsible for the operation of the *boutique*, they sometimes borrow money interest free from an older son or daughter in order to purchase merchandise, especially when either of them participates in the informal savings association (*sousou*) and receives the funds.

The family as a whole contributes to capital accumulation, and it is also responsible for any financial crisis that the store experiences. For example, we have noted elsewhere that the daily profits are what feed the family. Unless the credit given to clients and money spent for family needs are closely monitored, the *boutique* may suffer financial hardships or even bankruptcy.

As a family enterprise, the *boutique* provides at least one member of the family with a full-time job. It allows the family easy access to cash on a daily basis and makes available food items for possible family consumption. It positions the family somewhat above the rest of the neighbourhood. Owning a *boutique* is a distinction, a sign of higher social status in the community.

LIFE HISTORY OF A BOUTIQUE

Each *boutique* has its own life history. Sometimes it encompasses more than one generation, and during its life cycle it may go through several transformations. In the beginning a *boutique* is likely to be a small operation, catering to the basic needs of the people. With time and the changing face of the neighbourhood, the residents develop new needs, which will be reflected in the *boutique*'s stock.

The second phase in the life history of the *boutique* corresponds to the period when a certain stability is achieved. During that phase, the decision is made about what to sell and the best way to arrange the products on the shelves. The owner soon learns that it is more practical to place in the remotest corner of the *boutique* those objects that are not in constant demand and to place non-food items together. At the same time he or she learns to place items that are constantly in demand and also to have a corner in the room where extra stock can be piled up near the counter. The *boutique* reaches its highest peak of development during this period.

As they age, the owners have less energy to spend keeping up the *boutique* and may rather sell those items that are most in demand. The *boutique* provides them with a social life, a form of semi-retirement, and an extra income. This phase marks the period of decline of the *boutique*. At this time a daughter or son may move in and take over the operation, especially if one of the parents has died. With the new owner the *boutique* may again develop toward a new peak, and later experience another decline.

SOCIOECONOMIC FUNCTIONS

The socioeconomic functions of the *boutique* make it a well integrated unit in the neighbourhood. The manager's relationships with the neighbourhood encompass more than the economic arena; they are social and political as well. He or she links the community to the rest of society.

The relationship between the client and the shop owner is a very personal one. The *boutique* plays a role of provisioning the *quartier*. The slum dwellers go there for four reasons: first, because it is nearby and of easy access; second, because it offers a credit line; third, because most of the merchandise is sold on a subretail basis – for example, one may want to buy one cigarette, instead of a pack; and fourth, because it sells as a *dépanneur* ordinary things one needs to run a household. In contrast to the *boutique* the dwellers of the *quartier* must take their cars or use public transportation to go to the public produce market or to the butcher's shop. They naturally visit these places less regularly than the *boutique*.

The *boutique*, as mentioned, also has a political function in the neighbourhood. The shop owner is one of the key neighbourhood players in the mayoral elections. Previously the shop was where residents congregated to hear a candidate's speech. It was also the shop owner who held the stock (textile, rum, shoes) that was given away to induce individuals to vote for a particular candidate. That form of bribery is no longer practised; but politicians continue to use some strategic *boutiques* to hold neighbourhood meetings. It was in one of the grocery stores in Volga Plage that the mayor's representative held meetings during the most recent campaign. The *boutique* manager is a local politician who explains the candidate's platform to clients, makes good propaganda, and recruits new voters. The owner may try to influence votes during the electoral campaign for the mayor's office, thus becoming, like the shop, an instrument of the politics and policies of the mayor. The owner can 'badmouth' anyone who holds a public office because he has a ready-made clientele. A candidate who had all the shop owners against him or her would probably have a difficult time getting elected.

The *boutique*, then, brings in revenues and offers employment to the family. In addition to the owner, a son or daughter is also employed as a part-time helper or stand-in to allow the owner to do errands and take care of personal needs.

The *boutique* owner has also a social role as the one who gathers and distributes the news about the sick in the neighbourhood. Instead of going to the sick person's house, residents ask the shop owner and when someone knows a remedy for a given illness, the information is passed on through the shop owner to the person who needs it.

The shop owner knows all the people in the neighbourhood who buy from the *boutique* for cash or credit: their addresses, their financial status, their activities, and often their past history. It is as if he or she kept a file cabinet for the entire neighbourhood, the curriculum vitae of every individual. Much of the ongoing gossip here is fed through that particular source. The permanent observer of the neighbourhood, he or she is the *Journal Parlé* of the *quartier* as well as the knowledgeable informant. Because of their awareness, shop owners are often used by outsiders, politicians and others – as informants.

The *boutique* is the place where people congregate to gossip and enjoy themselves, and a place of rendezvous. It is where one comes to contrast one's interpretation of events with those of others. Here, one is assured of being aware of what is happening in the city. Thus the *boutique* facilitates a flow of communication among clients and between them and the shop owner.

It is also where one learns about the life situations of other people in the neighbourhood. One learns, for example, who do not pay their debts, when the shop owner is complaining about unpaid bills as a way of showing the prospective client that the business is no longer profitable. This information may be given when the owner is asked about the whereabouts of a specific client and replies 'I have not seen him for weeks, because he owes me some money'. If a client is sick or is going through a divorce, the owner may provide this information. The clients learn about one another through listening to what the owner has to say about every one of them.

The retail shop is a place where one seeks advice on family and legal matters. He or she is supposed to have acquired much practical knowledge from listening to so many different clients. While he may have the ability to keep a family together through his counsel, the shop owner is above all a gossip.

People spend time in front of the *boutique*, depending on factors such as the character of the shop owner, who may or may not tolerate the shop's being used as a hangout. An unfriendly owner may be able to keep the people at bay.

Young men especially congregate to talk to the daughter of the owner when she operates the store. Others come to check out other young women who may pass by the store.

The owner may try to protect his clients when the police are looking for them, and may refuse to tell the whereabouts of an individual if this is likely to cause trouble to his store. This may be the case if he is involved with them in selling drugs or if he buys contraband merchandise from them.

People leave messages for each other at the store. The owner may not remember everybody's name, but he remembers their addresses. He knows, further, what apartments are vacant and who the landlord is. He may be able to refer the individual who is looking for an apartment to the interested landlord.

REPRODUCTION OF POVERTY

The relation of the *boutique* to the dominant sector of society is asymmetrical and based on exploitation. The shop is located in a hierarchy of positions and its structural position in this hierarchy results from and reflects its inferior status and its position *vis-à-vis* the wholesale business community. Its own existence is shaped by its dependence on the wholesalers. It does not enjoy any distinct autonomy. Asymmetry results also because it is a poor person's business, characterised by lack of capital and lack of diversified manpower and resources, in an inferior or dependent position in the larger system. The reproduction of the total system does not change the asymmetry of the equation, nor the exploitative role played by the *boutique* in the local community.

The experience acquired in the running of a family enterprise such as the *boutique* includes a kind of managerial skill that one may use in running the household. There is a correlation between the *boutique* as a part of the reproduction of capital and the family contribution to the reproduction of poverty in the neighbourhood. The ability to reproduce the *boutique* as a unit of exploitation is linked to the daily reproduction of the family household as a consuming and labouring unit.

The *boutique*'s economic weakness rests in the fact that the manager learns the ropes on the job and the workers are family members. The owner is an entrepreneur, the central person, who takes on a series of functions that in a larger operation could be divided among various people. The owner is basically the principal salesman, the advertiser, the bookkeeper, the market specialist, and the purchaser. In addition employers and employees are recruited from within the limits of the family, which points to another weakness of the system in that the pool of specialist workers is too limited.

The limits of the *boutique* are expressed in the fact that no preparation is made for expansion – on site or by way of duplication, with the primal *boutique* as headquarters and the branches located elsewhere. Like any entrepreneur the *boutique* owner is a risk taker: one, however, with a limited vision of profit. The *boutique* owner is by no means a reckless capitalist.

The *boutique* is an instrument of the exploitation of the slum dwellers. It is the place that eats up their money. The exploitation materialises at the retail level, where the shop owner's profit is added to the profit already taken by the wholesaler. One can buy items with fixed prices at the supermarket, but here the price is flexible and seldom below that of the supermarket.

The system of credit makes the people dependent on the owner. Although they come in to buy the basics, credit serves as an incentive to buy more. Credit by itself is not a negative investment; it becomes so when it allows one to buy more than one is capable of paying for. The *boutique* is the local link to the national economic system of exploitation. It serves as an extension of the wholesale business. The owner exploits the people for his own profit. He is the last link in the chain of the exploitation process.

Although the *boutique* plays a series of social functions in the community, fundamentally it is a place where the people are exploited on a daily basis. It is here that exploitation wears a recognisable human face.

NOTES

1. Letchimy (1984, p. 127) explains the rural origins of the neighbourhood *boutique* as an economic and social institution and its functional role among lower-class urbanites. He sees the credit system as an extension of a rural practice. He notes that 'plusieurs familles du quartier possèdent un carnet de crédit pour s'approvisionner et le règlement se fait en fin de mois, à la réception du mandat de la "caisse d'allocations familiales", du salaire ou de la rémunération pour les "jobs" effectués. Ce type d'activité de crédit est issu des pratiques du milieu rural ou les dettes étaient gagées sur le bétail. Dans le milieu urbain le prolongement du commerce boutiquier de crédit répond dans une certaine mesure aux spécificités des ménages, plus particulièrement dans les quartiers insalubres où les revenus sont précaires et incertains. Cette pratique est aussi encourageante par l'absence d'appareillage électro-ménager pouvant permettre de stocker la marchandise achetée en gros. Dans ces conditions, l'acheteur s'approvisionne au fur et à mesure de ses besoins pour la journée et parfois même pour un repas.'

2. Letchimy (1984, p. 142) details for us the role of the site of the *boutique* in the organisation of neighbourhood space: 'Les *boutiques* des quartiers sont situées le plus souvent à un point de convergence. Elles servent de repères spatiaux. Le plus souvent, elles servent aussi de lieu de rencontre, d'animation et de rassemblement. Chaque *boutique* peut constituer un élément polarisant du quartier. Tout le monde se reconnait à partir de la *boutique* de Monsieur ou Madame . . . . L'ensemble de ces *boutiques* dessine dans l'espace une structure basée sur les aires de chalandise de chaque unité. Lorsqu'une *boutique* de plus grande importance vient s'installer, l'espace homogène créé par les *boutiques* se trouve éclaté et la notion d'appartenance et de reconnaissance. Il s'étiole dans une configuration plus vaste de l'espace que les résidants se donnent à partir de la grande surface créée' (Letchimy, 1984, p. 142).

3. Réaud (1977, p. 1) pinpoints the reasons why the *boutique* owner does not make large profits. He notes that the *boutique* owner 'n'achète que par petites quantités; il ne bénéficie donc pas de conditions d'achat très avantageuses. D'autre part, ses moyens financiers étant limités, il achète souvent à crédit, ce qui augmente le prix de revient des produits' (Réaud, 1977, p.1).

6 Savings Associations

One of the strategies by which urban Martinicans accumulate capital and save money is by participation in the rotating credit association known as the 'sousou'.[1] From the upper class to the lower, all kinds of urban Martinicans take an active part in this association. The *sousou* is a rotating savings and credit association that, unlike the regular, state-licensed bank, does not add interest charges to the borrowed capital. The money is not invested by the local organiser, but rather is given to each participant when it is his or her turn to benefit. In other words there is never enough money for the association to invest profitably; instead each individual is responsible for investing or otherwise using the money as he feels best. Another characteristic element of the *sousou* is that money is given to each participant following a specific order of rotation. To understand the system as such, we must focus on its internal organisation, including its mode of recruiting members, its functioning, the mechanisms by which it solves emerging problems, authority patterns, the meaning of exchanges, and the social ecology and trajectory of the *sousou* from one cycle to another. Those issues will be discussed in the present chapter, and they will shed light on another aspect of the reproduction of poverty in urban Martinique.

Mutual aid is recognised as the fundamental rationale of this association. Nevertheless we must not overlook its importance as a social institution, while keeping in mind its economic foundation. For Soen and De Comarond (1972, p. 1171) rotating savings associations are 'a form of small credit, a sort of self-created banking facility' and 'should therefore be regarded as a particular case of a mutual-help association'.

One can but agree with Kurtz (1973, p. 57) when he notes that 'the rotating credit association represents a socioeconomic adaptation to a condition of poverty and this condition forces poor people to make alternative adaptation outside of the national institutional matrix in order to ensure their survival'. The rotating credit association is not intended to uproot poverty – although it can sometimes be a pathway of upward mobility – but to ameliorate the burden of poverty. Oscar Lewis (1961, p. xxvii) tends to see it as part of the subculture: 'Many of the traits of the subculture of poverty can be viewed as attempts at local solutions for problems not met by existing institutions and agencies

113

. . . . For example, unable to obtain credit from banks they are thrown upon their own resources and organise informal credit devices without interest.' In this chapter the rotating credit association will be viewed as an institution that helps the urban dweller to cope with poverty and that is also a contributing factor to the reproduction of poverty in the lower-class neighbourhoods of Fort-de-France.

THE *SOUSOU* AS A SAVINGS ASSOCIATION

The participation of the urban dweller in a rotating credit association produces two interrelated phenomena. On the one hand as a source of cash it helps the poor to meet their daily consumption needs and thus to reproduce their daily existences. On the other hand as a source of capital it feeds and helps to reproduce the larger system of inequality. These tend to be fundamental features of the *sousou* as a savings institution.

The *sousou* is a savings association based on the rotation and distribution of the capital to each member according to a prescribed order.[2] In the process of putting a *sousou* in place a series of mechanisms must be elaborated for the selection and formation of the group, the order of rotation and distribution of the capital, the amount of money decided on, and the time factor.

The mechanism of formation is more than simply the process of recruitment. It more often includes the desire and ability of one individual to initiate the process just when it coincides with the need of others. This person must be able to approach people who are in need of money and to convince them to participate. Although the initiative may come from a leader who is also in need, it may rise from a general consensus of the group. It responds to the desire of the members of the group to satisfy their needs. A *sousou* with a leader-founder is *cephalous*; one with no individual head is *acephalous*. Solving one's own problems is not the only reason to join a *sousou*. Some participate in order to help others. My own analysis seems to corroborate Cope and Kurtz's finding that the individuals most likely to participate in rotating credit associations are those who want either to accumulate capital or to help relatives or friends (Cope and Kurtz 1980, p. 214).

The notion of authority or leadership is central to the organisation and functioning of most *sousou*. The initiator is the leader of the group, the central person to whom everyone is connected. Theoretically, since every participant has money in it, one would assume that the highest degree of solidarity and interaction in the *sousou* will be among the members. In practice the interaction is often vertical rather than horizontal – an interaction between each participant and the head of the group, and not the interaction among various equal members. What is important to participants is the reconnaissance factor. If one is accepted, one is recognised by others as being a good risk. The question whether to participate in a *sousou* is a decision made about a certain risk. To accept is one's positive answer that the risk is in some sense under control.

In actuality the risk of default is very much reduced, because members participate also in the selection of partners, as well as relying on the judgment of the leader of the group. Every participant is therefore known by at least one other member, who shares the responsibility on his or her behalf by engaging his own money. Before one joins such an association, one must assure oneself that the other participants have a source of income and are reliable, and that there is some contingency mechanism in case of default.

MODES OF RECRUITMENT

The recruitment process is the mechanism that helps to indicate the class status of each individual participant and the *sousou* as a group. In other words recruitment helps to distinguish those who belong to large capital-share *sousous* from those in small capital-share *sousous*. It is a process of differentiation and stratification, in which the participants are assigned a place in a hierarchy of positions. Those who join a poor people's *sousou* use the institution to reproduce their daily life; they do not gain access to the kinds of contacts that benefit members of an upper middle-class *sousou*. The environment of opportunities is simply not the same. The following description of the various modes of recruitment explains how the *sousous* in which the city-dweller participates tend more often than not to recruit people of similar social classes.

The recruitment process by which members are selected to join the association is central in the formation of the *sousou*. Seven modes of recruitment are used. In the first mode an initiator looks for people in his environment as possible members. This is a period of probing and testing, during which possible members learn about other people's willingness to join. This mode of recruitment is by invitation, but an invitation does not mean automatic acceptance. Most likely the person approached will inquire about the other members. Each person recruited at the beginning of the process becomes therefore a founding member of the association.

The second mode of recruitment is by self-invitation. The individual who organises a *sousou* is not doing it as an outsider, but rather with the expectation of being part of it. This person will also be a founding member, but has recruited himself or herself rather than accepted an invitation from another.

The third mode of recruitment is by way of replacement. Here the member is not invited at the beginning of the process but only afterward when a problem arises – for example, the default or death of another. Persons who join a *sousou* that is already in rotation have minimal input into its organisation, since the principles of rotation and distribution have been agreed on before they come in.

The fourth mode is to be recruited as the associate of an existing member. The new person may not be known to the entire membership, but shares dues with the others and receives part of the capital at an appropriate time in the rotation.

The fifth mode of recruitment is by informal inquiry and application. If someone hears of the formation of a *sousou* in the neighbourhood and asks to be part of it, it is likely that the members will accept the application and will try to be accommodating.

The sixth mode of recruitment is by consensus. This mode is found only in the singular case of the *sousou* without a head. At the yard level neighbours may decide to form a *sousou*, and nobody is really in charge since they know each other and live next door to each other. A similar process occurs in the formation of the family *sousou*. Each member receives in turn the money the other members have separately contributed. In this instance no one takes the initiative of inviting the others; they have simply come together to form a *sousou* by consensus.

Recruitment is also done in the seventh mode by indirect invitation. In this case the head invites existing members to find other members. When the initiator invites, the person is accepted immediately, whereas when a member invites someone, the choice has to be approved by the organiser. For that matter not all of those invited by a member will receive the approval of the organiser or of the other participants.

During the recruitment process, one point discussed is that of the money that must be contributed during the cycle of the rotation. Deciding the exact amount is a process of selection in itself, because people will use this variable in making the decision to join or not to join the association. The amount requested may be excessive in relation to one's salary, or too small as a function of one's hopes and needs. Those who adhere to the *sousou* are likely to be individuals who are able to pay the dues and whose needs can be met by the association. However, while the rotation and distribution of the fund may be discussed at the initial level, the final arrangements may not be made before the full membership has been selected.

ROTATION AND DISTRIBUTION

Rotation and distribution of the fund's shares are part of the process by which poverty is reproduced, simply because they ensure the survival of the social group. They are essential to the orderly operation of the rotating credit system, for they strengthen the participants' awareness of their rights and obligations. The members themselves must agree about the direction of the rotation. The variable of individual need is of utmost importance in choosing positions in the rotation. If the members disapprove of the way their positions have been assigned, they will set up a lottery. Logistical problems are discussed, such as how the money should be given, when and how often, who will collect the fund, and who will distribute it to the members. Each individual wants to know exactly where he or she is situated in the chain and what is expected during the rotation. The notion of distribution follows that of rotation, and the rotation is a function of the distribution of the fund. The money goes from one hand to another until the end of the cycle.

Time is another factor taken into consideration. The time of contribution will not necessarily coincide with times of distribution. In that respect the Mexican experience of rotating credit is somewhat similar to the Martinican. 'Nor do contributions and the allocation of fund shares have to occur at the same time', Velez-Ibanez (1983, p. 39) writes. 'Contributions can be made weekly and the fund share allocated monthly.' This is likely to be the pattern when individuals receive a bi-weekly or weekly salary and are unable or unwilling to expend a large portion of weekly income for such a venture. Allocation and contribution may, however, occur at the same time if it will save the participant a trip. One who does not work in the same office or live in the same neighbourhood as the organiser saves both time and money by not having to take the bus, or drive, once to contribute and again to collect a share of the money.

INTERNAL ORGANISATION OF THE *SOUSOU*

Although we may agree that the rotating credit association is in general a contributing factor to the reproduction of poverty, we must add that there are several forms of *sousou*, each catering to people with different expectations and needs. A discussion of the various models follows. Interviews with informants from Terres-Sainville, Volga Plage, and Sainte Thérèse, three neighbourhoods of Fort-de-France, support the conclusion that the people in urban Martinique participate in seven different types of *sousou*. Each form corresponds to a strategy the poor have devised to adapt in their milieu. It is necessary to study each type and its function in the informal economy of the neighbourhoods.

Model 1: The Acephalous 'Sousou'

In this structure there is no individual who serves as head or secretary of the organisation (see Figure 6.1). One is most likely to find this kind

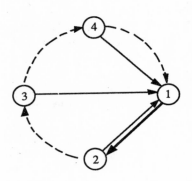

1,2,3,4	Individual members
→	Money contributed to common fund
←	Money distributed to member
⌐	Rotation of distribution

FIGURE 6.1 Acephalous *Sousou*.

of arrangement at the level of family or yard, because it requires that each member know the others well. Every week or month members return their agreed-on contribution to the participant to which it belongs at that turn. What is specific in this model is that the member who receives the capital is not called on to make an effort that week, but may or may not choose to do so.

Model 2: A 'Sousou' with a Treasurer

Probably the most common form of *sousou* in urban Martinique is that in which an individual acts as the head or treasurer of the unit, and the money is given to the treasurer, who in return gives it to the member to

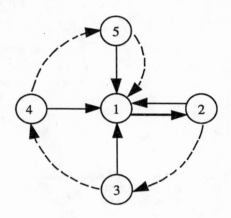

1	President
2,3,4,5	Other members
→	Money contributed to common fund
←	Money distributed to member
⌒	Rotation of distribution

FIGURE 6.2 *Sousou* with a Treasurer.

whom it belongs at each turn (see Figure 6.2). The treasurer has to collect the sum from each participating member. The treasurer is central in the functioning of the *sousou*; as the initiator, he or she is the one who knows everyone else and may have some special relations with each member.

The following example is an interesting variation of Model 2. A woman who is not a participating member of the association serves as an intermediary between the treasurer and the members who work in the building where she is a supervisor. She has been for many years the initiator of several other *sousous*

TABLE 6.1 DDASS *Sousou*

Date of Contribution and Allocation	Name of Participants	Workplace
30 April 1985	Jeanne	DDASS*
30 May 1985	Margareth	DDASS
30 June 1985	Jocelyne	COTOREP†
30 July 1985	Yvette	COTOREP
30 August 1985	Solange	DDASS
30 September 1985	Michelle	DDASS
30 October 1985	Antoinette	DDASS
30 November 1985	Marie	COTOREP
30 December 1985	André	COTOREP
30 January 1986	Mireille	COTOREP

Note: Fictitious names are used with actual name of workplace to avoid revealing the identity of the participants.
*DDASS = Direction Départementale de l'Action Sanitaire et Sociale.
†COTOREP = Commission Technique d'Orientation et de Reclassement Professionnel.

In this *sousou* (see Table 6.1) each participant is asked to contribute 500 francs before or on the thirtieth of each month. This *sousou* has three specific features. (1) It is a mixed *sousou* in that participants belong to two different offices or workplaces. (2) For each group there is a person in charge of collecting the due. In the COTOREP group the treasurer, so to speak, is a member of the *sousou*, while in the DDASS the treasurer is a trustworthy individual who is not a contributing member. This leads to the observation that one may play a leadership role in a *sousou* without contributing or receiving money from the association. (3) In this *sousou*, except for one man, the participating members are females.

Model 3: A 'Sousou' with Double Membership

There is no informal law that forbids one to hold a double membership in a *sousou*. In fact some individuals pay two shares and consequently appear twice during the rotation (see Figure 6.3). This is a strategy that adapts an informal economic activity to individual needs. It is used when one has obligations that cannot be met by participating in two different *sousous* because of the difficulty of situating oneself to advantage in two rotation processes. Double memberships also occur when one has more money to share than the amount agreed on by the membership. Willingness to buy two shares gives one more flexibility in choosing a place in the cycle. The disadvantage that one contributes more than others in the rotation is offset by the fact that one receives the funds more often than the other members.

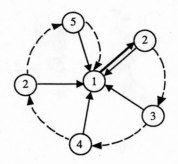

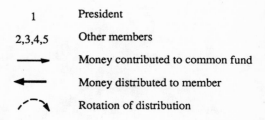

1	President
2,3,4,5	Other members
⟶	Money contributed to common fund
⟵	Money distributed to member
⟋ ⟍	Rotation of distribution

FIGURE 6.3 *Sousou* with Double Membership.

Model 4: A 'Sousou' with Associate Membership

One may want to participate in a *sousou* but be unable to pay the total amount of the required contribution. The structure makes some allowance for partnerships (see Figure 6.4). Members may decide to share with friends. In a typical arrangement one member pays half and the associate member pays the other half. The entire membership may be unaware of this arrangement, including the treasurer. Partnership does not create any problem so long as the full amount is paid on time. When it is their turn to receive the capital, the partners each get half. Thus partnership permits one to save money according to one's financial situation.

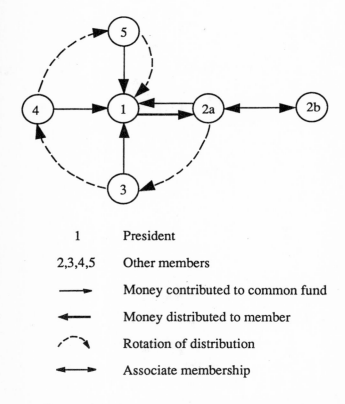

1	President
2,3,4,5	Other members
⟶	Money contributed to common fund
⟵	Money distributed to member
⤳	Rotation of distribution
⟷	Associate membership

FIGURE 6.4   *Sousou* with Associate Membership.

Model 5: A 'Sousou' Network

Here we find two or more *sousous* connected to each other by the fact that one or more members participate simultaneously in both. These *sousous* are defined in terms of the position of the members in each one. Mathematically speaking there are three different arrangements. In the first structure (see Figure 6.5) the same person serves as a treasurer in both *sousous*. He or she may arrange to receive money from both groups at the same time or at different times.

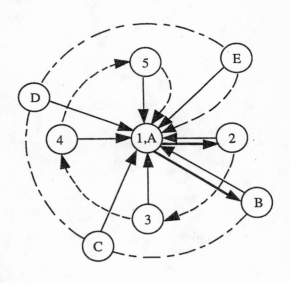

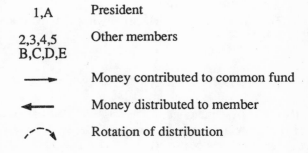

1,A	President
2,3,4,5 B,C,D,E	Other members
⟶	Money contributed to common fund
⟵	Money distributed to member
⌒	Rotation of distribution

FIGURE 6.5 *Sousou* Network.

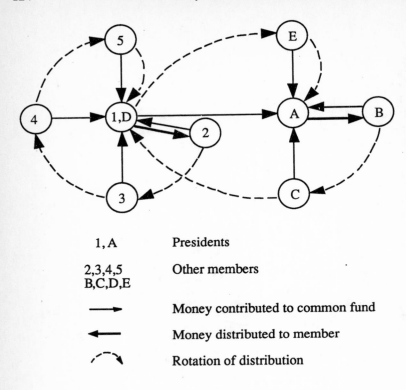

1, A	Presidents
2,3,4,5 B,C,D,E	Other members
⟶	Money contributed to common fund
⟵	Money distributed to member
⌒➘	Rotation of distribution

FIGURE 6.6 *Sousou* Network.

One person may be both the head of a *sousou* and an active member in another *sousou* (Figure 6.6).

Members may be active in both *sousous* without playing a leadership role (Figure 6.7).

FUNCTIONAL ADAPTATION

One of the objective functions of the rotating credit association is to provide the poor with the means of survival. In the economic sphere it makes the reproduction of poverty possible. The use of the *sousou* is widespread in the poor neighbourhoods of Fort-de-France and associations are organised at many different levels, from the family

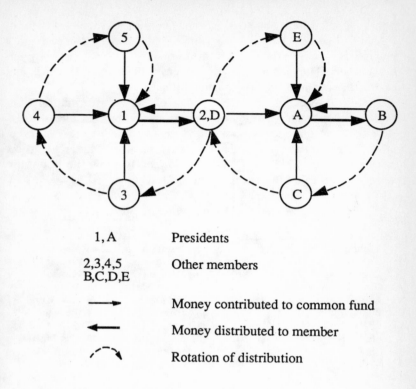

1, A	Presidents
2,3,4,5 B,C,D,E	Other members
$\longrightarrow$	Money contributed to common fund
$\longleftarrow$	Money distributed to member
$\overset{\frown}{}$	Rotation of distribution

FIGURE 6.7   *Sousou* Network.

unit to the workplace. In fact there are individuals who participate in *sousous* at several levels. The family *sousou* meets certain routine needs, and participation in *sousous* at the workplace corresponds to other types of needs.

The functional adaptation of the *sousou* can be appreciated in terms of the amount of money agreed on and the choice of partners. For that matter there is a *sousou* for every taste and one may join any of them according to one's pocketbook.

The *sousou* is not a prefabricated structure, but is shaped by the people who adhere to it. This is clearer when one looks at its life cycle. A *sousou* may be terminated at the end of the first cycle for any reason; it is basically a 'one cycle' institution. Terms must be renegotiated for a new cycle to begin. In fact at the end of a cycle there are several different possibilities. The members may continue with a new cycle if they decide to do so. They may also make some changes. For example, they may decide on a different rotation, a new amount of money, or new members. The inauguration of a new cycle will depend on both the new and the old needs of the participants.

The following examples give an idea of the transformation that occurs in membership from one cycle to another. As one *sousou* completes its rotation and begins a new one the membership is not the same. Three *sousou* in which workers in the Mayor's Office participated from 1983 and 1984 to 1985 clearly show the mutation from one cycle to another (see Table 6.2).

TABLE 6.2   *Mayor's Office Sousou*

	1983	1984	1985
1.	Monconthour	Monconthour	Rabathalie
2.	Crétineau	Crétineau	Monconthour
3.	Jean Louis	Rochambeau	Saximant
4.	Ilmany	Louis Marie	Chilise
5.	Humat	Pamphile	Louis Marie
6.	Danglade	Honoré	Crétineau
7.	Crétineau (replaced Caddy)	Ladic	Dortane
8.	Guillon	Nagaradini	Louis Marie
9.	Six	Souchette	Marcel
10.	Guillon	Cadignon	Saximant
11.	Telga	Zadi	Nagaradini
12.	—	—	Rabathalie

In the *sousou* of 1983, No. 7 was replaced in the course of the rotation by No. 2, and another participant held two memberships, Nos. 8 and 10. Monconthour, No. 1, and Crétineau, No. 2, who continued to participate in the *sousous* of 1984 and 1985, put themselves in positions where they made positive returns on their money. Monconthour placed himself twice in the first position and once in the second position. Crétineau placed herself twice in second position and once in the sixth position.

In the *sousou* of 1984 Rochambeau no longer worked at the Mayor's Office but had another government job. He was allowed to continue to participate in the *sousou*. Four of the 1983 participants continued as members of the 1985 *sousou* but with different positions in the rotation.

The *sousou* of 1985, which was a carry-over from 1983 and 1984, shows three individuals with double membership. Only four people are newly recruited. Those in first and third position are also found in tenth and twelfth position.

The fact that there are so many forms of the *sousou* allows room for flexibility, because the different structures are elastic with respect to the schedule of payments. The periodicity of payments matches that of members' wages and salaries. For example, employees of the local government join *sousou* demanding monthly contributions, while others may participate in weekly *sousous*.

THE *SOUSOU* AS A PROBLEM-SOLVING INSTITUTION

Participation in a *sousou* could be detrimental to the effort by the poor to accumulate capital if the members defaulted. In my study of the reproduction of poverty in the poor neighbourhoods, default of such associations did not emerge as a routine problem. The following discussion attempts to show why it is not.

Although much effort is expended in choosing the most suitable and problem-free individuals to participate in the *sousou*, there are additionally some mechanisms built in to meet any problems which may arise. The nature of the problem will determine the specific solutions.

It is always a possibility that someone will run away with the money and leave everyone in a mess. However, none of my informants knew of such an occurrence. I have not been able to find a single case where this had happened. It remains, of course, a theoretical possibility.

There is also the continual risk that an individual who has received funds will decide not to continue paying in. It is to avoid this situation that such great care is taken in the selection of members. They must be very reliable people, sometimes friends; they must produce references that they are capable of paying their dues. This is one reason most *sousous* are run on a twelve-month cycle – from January to December, for example; but even with all these precautions, the groups encounter problems once in a while. Since the institution is illegal, there is no possible recourse to the court; but even if nothing can be done through the formal judiciary system, there are ways and means in the informal legal system. It is possible to put pressure on members of the individual's family, or to threaten his or her reputation. Usually a defaulter's parents pay to avoid trouble.

The organiser of a *sousou* may not know every member of the association very well. Some members will have been recruited by others as time goes on. Although much care was taken initially, the leader may have slight doubts about one of two members' ability to pay on time. For that reason the leader will place less trustworthy individuals at the end of the cycle, and they end up being the last to get the fund shares.

If a member decides to leave a *sousou* before the end of the rotation, it is customary for that member to ask a friend to take his place. If, however, a replacement cannot be found then the membership may share his dues and therefore receive a greater return without having to interrupt the rotation. The membership may also invite someone else to replace the withdrawing member, or one of the remaining members may take a second share, so as to get the funds twice during a rotation (see Table 6.3). At each such juncture, monetary adjustment may be in order to keep the rotation moving. An informant reports, 'My mother was the initiator of a *sousou* and one of the members died. My mother and another member each contributed half the dues of the deceased, and when they received the funds each got half. In that way, they solved the rotation problem.' If an individual member is having financial difficulty, other members will help him to pay the dues, and when he or she receives the funds, they will share with those who helped.

In one *sousou* I learned of, the association had to replace a member who emigrated to Paris in the middle of the rotation cycle. In this case there was no need to call on someone else to replace the person who was leaving the island. One of the participants simply filled in by taking over the membership.

ADVANTAGES AND DISADVANTAGES

Although there are advantages in being part of a *sousou*, there are also disadvantages, negative factors working against the ability of the poor to accumulate capital. The persistence of the practice of *sousou* at all social levels in Martinique attests to its functional adaptation. To survive over the years, it must have played an important economic and social role: in other words, the advantages must have outweighed the disadvantages.

We have touched on some of the disadvantages, especially the risk of default. As mentioned earlier, there are mechanisms through which that risk can be defused. From a psychological point of view, default is always a nuisance. It may or may not be intentional. Default can result

TABLE 6.3   *Default in Sousou*

Months	Participants
July	Jeanne
August	Joséphine
September	Michelle
October	Marlène
November	Micheline
December	Monique
January	Violaine was replaced in October by Monique who now holds two memberships

from illness or death or simply because a member has walked away with the fund (see also Cope and Kurtz 1980, p. 215).

When we study the phenomenon of *sousou* as an investment, two major problems are apparent. The first is that *sousou* is a passive way of saving, in contrast to a bank, and especially for the last persons in the rotation cycle. For these participants the money is simply set aside with no interest earned. It is evident that if the same amount of money were placed in a regular bank, they would have received both capital and interests. The greater the amount the greater the difference in terms of opportunity lost.

The second problem concerns the treasurer. In order to collect the funds and reimburse the members, this person will probably have to make a few telephone calls at a franc each and use his car and gas, expenses that are not paid for by the membership. The treasurer will use his own money to pay for these expenses to make sure that the rotation is smooth.

The advantages are far more numerous than the disadvantages. Informants often say that the *sousou* forces them to save money, since they must find means to provide their monthly contributions. The saving is more difficult because of the spirit of consumption that pervades the entire society. One informant says 'Each time I receive a *sousou* I had a project. I bought a lawnmower; another time, I paid a loan on my car. I always chose to be at the end of the year because my insurances were going to end in November. Also at the end of the year, I was able to buy gifts for family members and friends.'

One is forced to save because one has someone's money to reimburse. By contrast there is no obligation to save when one deals with a formal bank. The bank is indifferent to the way one chooses to use one's money. The *sousou* helps a great deal in planning one's budget in advance – it provides a kind of financial discipline through the constant necessity of reimbursing the partners.

One informant states that she used her return once to buy a kitchen and another time a refrigerator. She had participated in a weekly *sousou* with twenty-six members. Other individuals who have exhausted their credit in a regular bank may find it advantageous to get some extra cash from participating in a *sousou*.

THE PERIMETER OF THE *SOUSOU*

The study of the perimeter of the *sousou* illuminates one more element in the notion of the hierarchy of environments. The poor, whether at the workplace or the neighbourhood, belong to *sousous* organised by lower-class members of Martinican society. Their ability to use the association for upward mobility is very limited. The *sousou* is limited in both time and space. It begins with the first rotation and ends up with the last on a weekly, bi-weekly, or monthly basis. The number of participants determines the length of the cycle. The *sousou* tends to function within a one-year period: it can be any length, but not longer than a year. I was unable to find a *sousou* that went beyond a year in its rotation.

There are natural niches for the *sousou*. The most elementary structure of *sousou* is found among families. The second niche for the organisation of *sousou* is the yard, that compound that is the basis of operation for the extended family, but incorporates other members as well. The neighbourhood is another niche in the same category. The third niche is the workplace. Individuals who work for the same institution do organise *sousous* among themselves, including individuals of the same profession, or employees of the same firm or institution. There exist, for example, *sousous* of taxi drivers or street vendors. Whereas the *sousous* described above are geographically situated, *sousou* whose membership is made up of friends and acquaintances are not. This form of *sousou* does not have a territorial epicentre; all the members have one point of convergence, the initiator. However, the categories described are not mutually exclusive. A workplace-based *sousou* may incorporate other people as well, and the same is true for the yard *sousou*. These various niches explain the logical order in the recruitment and composition of *sousou*. For each of them the presence of exogenous elements can be explained in terms of the exhaustion of the niche. Once all the people of that niche have been recruited, if the *sousou* needs more members, then other people will be invited to fill the need.

People who used to belong to a *sousou* in the workplace may continue to join them even when they have retired. One informant speaks of a lady who used to participate in a *sousou* organised by employees of City Hall and was allowed to continue her participation even though she no longer works for the city. Without this invitation she would have had some problems finding a *sousou* that corresponds to her needs. State employees who during their retirement receive a monthly pension are in a better position to participate in a *sousou* than other employees of the private sector of the same status because they receive their pay cheques on a quarterly basis.

According to informants *sousous* are organised on a weekly, bi-weekly, or monthly basis. These are the periods during which the people have access to cash, either from their salaries or by other means.

THE FORMS OF THE EXCHANGE

The form of exchange is indicative of the social class of the participants. The poor trade in cash, whereas the members of bourgeois *sousou* trade in cheques as well. Since the goal of the persons who participate in *sousous* is to save money, it is useful to ask how the means of exchange affects that goal.

The *sousou* by definition is a monetary transaction in which the state does not take its usual share of taxes. The money is exchanged in two basic ways, depending largely on the amount of the transactions.

In the *sousou* in which dues per member do not exceed 50 francs (10 dollars) the money is commonly given in currency to the treasurer, who returns it to the winning member. It is a simple matter to handle the money in this way. However, *sousous* with larger dues transact business by cheque. Cheques may be issued either to the receiver or to the treasurer. One also finds *sousous* in which one or more members give cheques all at once to the treasurer for dues they will owe throughout the rotation. They are postdated cheques to be cashed only in the month for which they were written, not before. If a problem comes up, they can easily be cancelled or torn up. This procedure eliminates a series of inconveniences and renders the rotation fairly smooth.

SOUSOU IN THE STRUCTURE OF MARTINICAN SOCIETY

The *sousou* offers an interesting case of the functioning of an institution in the informal economy. It draws members who participate also in the formal economy in that some individuals who deal with regular banks also take part in *sousou*. It does not replace the formal banking system, it serves only as an additional way of saving money. It is unlikely that someone would withdraw his money from a bank to put it in a *sousou*, but it often happens that people use the *sousou* to accumulate capital in order to invest it in a bank. The *sousou* can even be said to play two roles in the formal banking system. It feeds the bank, and provides periodic cash so that depositors may not have to withdraw their money for occasional purchases.

Participating in the two systems gives the Martinican a short and long-range strategy. Whereas the formal bank provides a permanent backup and a credit line to sustain long-range plans, the *sousou* provides quick answers to emergencies or seasonal problems.

The *sousou* can at the same time be shown to have a negative impact on the formal banking system. The money contributed to the *sousou* is not necessarily invested in the bank, and people are not likely to take out a loan with interest charges from the bank if they can obtain a loan without interest through the *sousou*. From whatever angle one views the situation, a huge amount of money passes from hand to hand from which the state cannot take any bite.

The informal system is not completely without formal rules. There are many cases in which agreements are signed, rules stated, the membership list written down and known by everyone, and records of contribution and payment kept. Written rules are evidence for the evolution of the institution but they do not make it a formal institution. They do, however, render it more acceptable to educated people. The legality of such written rules has yet to be tested in the courts of law.

As Geertz (1962, p. 262) points out, the rotating credit association in developing countries is becoming a more and more bureaucratic institution. In Martinique, as we have seen, records are kept and skilled managers are called on whether or not they contribute financially to the association. In Geertz's (1962, p. 262) words, the rotating credit association is an economic institution with a specific function that behaves like a firm. This behaviour is the similarity and the link between the rotating credit association and the family. As kinds of firms, the linkage is economic in nature. The family invests in the *sousou* to accumulate and save money. The rotating credit association recruits family members to perpetuate its own existence and reduce the possibility for default.

The imbrication of the informal economy into the formal economy is here very much marked. For one thing it is the salary earned in the formal sector that is used for savings in the informal sector. The money saved in the informal sector is used to buy goods and services in the formal sector. We speak not of a parallel economy, but of one that is very much integrated in the formal economy.

The *sousou* appears in the folk culture of urban dwellers as a strategy for survival, chiefly because of its capacity for producing income; but the evolution of the meaning of *sousou* is linked to the history of the needs of the people. Whereas a few years ago, people participated in *sousou* to meet the most basic needs, now that Martinican society is so heavily consumerist, *sousous* are sometimes used to purchase luxury goods. There has also been evolution in the size of the fund, because of higher wages. It is evident that there is a correlation between the history of needs, the history of salaries, and the size of *sousou*. In other words, as salaries increase, Martinicans develop expensive tastes, and consequently form bigger *sousous* to meet these needs.

The *sousou* plays a part in the integration of society because it facilitates communication among members of several groups. Making in place a *sousou* requires getting in touch with different people and forming a group of followers of which one is a leader. Through *sousou*, groups are formed that may hold together for more than one cycle. Participation in *sousou* leads to new contacts and enlarges one's circle of relationships. The role of the initiator is strategic in keeping the group together.

Participation in *sousou* builds one's trust in the community. This is an important function in the case of the newcomer, who may not have the proper references: through the *sousou* he or she shows honesty and trustworthiness. *Sousou* affords an official recognition by the community. Particularly in the case of someone who has had a bad reputation, the opportunity to write off the debt to society is a benefit. Such an individual can use the *sousou* to rebuild the confidence of the community.

One's membership in a *sousou* may indicate one's social status simply through the amount of money one is requested to contribute. The cost of participation is sometimes a restrictive factor. The bourgeois participate in more expensive *sousous*, the urban poor in cheaper ones.

On the other hand, because friendship as well as **money is important** in the recruitment process, sometimes individuals may make an effort at stretching their purses so as to join a more prestigious *sousou*. As with any prestigious club, the individual who belongs to a *sousou* gains contacts that may be useful in the future. The association is, for some, a strategy for upward mobility. Velez-Ibanez (1983, p. 37) has found that urban Mexicans and Chicanos have developed a similar strategy. He writes that 'among some women in upper-middle or upper-class residential areas, the associations are a means by which to enter prestigious residential networks'. In the case of Martinique people may not have a sound economic base for participating in a costly *sousou*, except by straining their resources, but they do so with a view to making contacts and consequently upgrading their positions. We find lower-class individuals participating in middle-class *sousous* in the same way that middle-class people participate in upper-class *sousous*.

The *sousou* fosters financial solidarity among people of the same status. One is requested to participate not only to solve one's own needs, – people would probably find other ways to eke out their livelihoods – but as a way of helping others. By participating one creates the opportunity of requesting other members' help when one is in need. The notion of 'reciprocity' is important. One benefits by using someone's money without having to request a loan from a bank, and one expects to offer that person the same benefit at some later point.

The *sousou* functions at every level of Martinican society as a mechanism of sociocultural integration. It forms groups, encourages solidarity, and helps participants to meet their needs. Since the structure is dynamic, members leave continually and new ones are incorporated. Because different people act as initiators, individuals may find themselves drawn into new *sousous* with a different leader or membership.

REPRODUCTION OF POVERTY

The rotating credit association contributes in its own way to the reproduction of poverty in the neighbourhood. It reinforces the consumerism of Martinican society by providing instant cash to the participants. It is an institution of the capitalist system of production that gives the people at the bottom the illusion of participating in the accumulation of capital. It sustains the exploitative system to the extent that people use it to cope with poverty.

The structure is also exploitative from an economic standpoint. It permits members to exploit other members. Because the association is basically a one-cycle institution, some members reap the benefit from their position in the rotation. To prove that this is so, we need to do two things. First, we must calculate the interest a member would have earned if the money were placed in a bank instead of in a *sousou*. Second, we need to identify the positions in the rotation that theoretically provide a positive return on one's investment.

For the first step let us assume that the contribution is $100 per member per month, with twelve members for twelve months. Further assume the interest rate to be 10 per cent and that it will not be compounded during the entire cycle of the *sousou*. Earned interest is calculated according to the formula:

$$X = \frac{C x I x M}{Y}$$

X = earned interest
C = stands for capital
I = interest rate
M = the number of days in the month
Y = the number of days in the year

Tables 6.4 and 6.5 show quite clearly on a monthly basis what interest a participant earns or loses in taking part in a *sousou* instead of a formal bank. The individual who receives the funds in December would, if he placed $100 in a formal bank every month of the year, have accumulated an interest of $55.22. He has clearly lost an opportunity to earn extra dollars. Answer to our second query then becomes evident. The first six participants to get shares have a positive return on their investments; they receive interest-free loans from the membership. The other six have a negative return (see Table 6.6). It is to one's advantage to place oneself among the first six to receive the funds. Those who invest money gained in the *sousou* in a bank earn interest from using other people's money.

By participation in the *sousous* the poor end up providing no-interest loans to others. In this way they maintain the flow of capital, participate in their own exploitation, and contribute to the maintenance and reproduction of their own sphere of poverty.

TABLE 6.4   *Interest Gained or Lost Through Participation in Sousou: First Six Months (in $)*

	Jan	Feb	March	April	May	June	July	Aug	Sep	Oct	Nov	Dec
return of funds (on 1st)	1200											
funds contributed (on 1st)	100	100	100	100	100	100	100	100	100	100	100	100
cumulative own funds contr.	100											
loaned funds	−1100	−1000	−900	−800	−700	−600	−500	−400	−300	−200	−100	0
interest earned ea month	9.34	7.67	7.64	6.58	5.95	4.93	4.25	3.40	2.47	1.70	0.82	0.00
cumulative interest	9.34	17.01	24.66	31.23	37.18	42.11	46.36	49.75	52.22	53.92	54.74	54.74
return of funds (on 1st)		1200										
funds contributed (on 1st)	100	100	100	100	100	100	100	100	100	100	100	100
cumulative own funds contr.	100	200										
loaned funds		−1000	−900	−800	−700	−600	−500	−400	−300	−200	−100	0
interest (lost)/earned ea month	−0.85	7.67	7.64	6.58	5.95	4.93	4.25	3.40	2.47	1.70	0.82	0.00
cumulative interest	−0.85	6.82	14.47	21.04	26.99	31.92	36.16	39.56	42.03	43.73	44.55	44.55
return of funds (on 1st)			1200									
funds contributed (on 1st)	100	100	100	100	100	100	100	100	100	100	100	100
cumulative own funds contr.	100	200	300									
loaned funds			−900	−800	−700	−600	−500	−400	−300	−200	−100	0
interest (lost)/earned ea month	−0.85	−1.53	7.64	6.58	5.95	4.93	4.25	3.40	2.47	1.70	0.82	0.00
cumulative interest	−0.85	−2.38	5.26	11.84	17.78	22.71	26.96	30.36	32.82	34.52	35.34	35.34

return of funds (on 1st)				1200								
funds contributed (on 1st)	100	100	100	100	100	100	100	100	100	100	100	100
cumulative own funds contr.	100	200	300	400	500	600	700	800	900	1000	1100	1200
loaned funds				-800	-700	-600	-500	-400	-300	-200	-100	0
interest (lost)/earned ea month	-0.85	-1.53	-2.55	6.58	5.95	4.93	4.25	3.40	2.47	1.70	0.82	0.00
cumulative interest	-0.85	-2.38	-4.93	1.64	7.59	12.52	16.77	20.16	22.63	24.33	25.15	25.15

return of funds (on 1st)					1200							
funds contributed (on 1st)	100	100	100	100	100	100	100	100	100	100	100	100
cumulative own funds contr.	100	200	300	400	500	600	700	800	900	1000	1100	1200
loaned funds					-700	-600	-500	-400	-300	-200	-100	0
interest (lost)/earned ea month	-0.85	-1.53	-2.55	-3.29	5.95	4.93	4.25	3.40	2.47	1.70	0.82	0.00
cumulative interest	-0.85	-2.38	-4.93	-8.22	-2.27	2.66	6.90	10.30	12.77	14.47	15.29	15.29

return of funds (on 1st)						1200						
funds contributed (on 1st)	100	100	100	100	100	100	100	100	100	100	100	100
cumulative own funds contr.	100	200	300	400	500	600	700	800	900	1000	1100	1200
loaned funds						-600	-500	-400	-300	-200	-100	0
interest (lost)/earned ea month	-0.85	-1.53	-2.55	-3.29	-4.25	4.93	4.25	3.40	2.47	1.70	0.82	0.00
cumulative interest	-0.85	-2.38	-4.93	-8.22	-12.47	-7.53	-3.29	0.11	2.58	4.27	5.10	5.10

TABLE 6.5   *Interest Gained/Lost in Sousou: Second Six Months (in $)*

	Jan	Feb	March	April	May	June	July	Aug	Sep	Oct	Nov	Dec
return of funds (on 1st)							1200					
funds contributed (on 1st)	100	100	100	100	100	100	100	100	100	100	100	100
cumulative own funds contr.	100	200	300	400	500	600	700					
loaned funds							−500	−400	−300	−200	−100	0
interest (lost)/earned ea month	−0.85	−1.53	−2.55	−3.29	−4.25	−4.93	4.25	3.40	2.47	1.70	0.82	0.00
cumulative interest		−2.38	−4.93	−8.22	−12.47	−17.40	−13.15	−9.75	−7.29	−5.59	−4.77	−4.77
return of funds (on 1st)								1200				
funds contributed (on 1st)	100	100	100	100	100	100	100	100	100	100	100	100
cumulative own funds contr.	100	200	300	400	500	600	700	800				
loaned funds								−400	−300	−200	−100	0
interest (lost)/earned ea month	−0.85	−1.53	−2.55	−3.29	−4.25	−4.93	−5.95	3.40	2.47	1.70	0.82	0.00
cumulative interest		−2.38	−4.93	−8.22	−12.47	−17.40	−23.34	−19.95	−17.48	−15.78	−14.96	−14.96
return of funds (on 1st)									1200			
funds contributed (on 1st)	100	100	100	100	100	100	100	100	100	100	100	100
cumulative own funds contr.	100	200	300	400	500	600	700	800	900			
loaned funds									−300	−200	−100	0
interest (lost)/earned ea month	−0.85	−1.53	−2.55	−3.29	−4.25	−4.93	−5.95	−6.79	2.47	1.70	0.82	0.00
cumulative interest		−2.38	−4.93	−8.22	−12.47	−17.40	−23.34	−30.14	−27.67	−25.97	−25.15	−25.15

Block 1:

return of funds (on 1st)	100	100										
funds contributed (on 1st)	100	100	100	100	100	100	100	100	100	100	100	100
cumulative own funds contr.	100	200	300	400	500	600	700	800	900	1000	1100	1200
loaned funds										-200	-100	0
interest (lost)/earned ea month	-0.85	-1.53	-2.55	-3.29	-4.25	-4.93	-5.95	-6.79	-7.64	1.70	0.82	0.00
cumulative interest		-2.38	-4.93	-8.22	-12.47	-17.40	-23.34	-30.14	-37.78	-36.08	-35.26	-35.26

Block 2:

return of funds (on 1st)	100	100										
funds contributed (on 1st)	100	100	100	100	100	100	100	100	100	100	100	100
cumulative own funds contr.	100	200	300	400	500	600	700	800	900	1000	1100	1200
loaned funds											-100	0
interest (lost)/earned ea month	-0.85	-1.53	-2.55	-3.29	-4.25	-4.93	-5.95	-6.79	-7.40	-8.49	0.82	0.00
cumulative interest		-2.38	-4.93	-8.22	-12.47	-17.40	-23.34	-30.14	-37.53	-46.03	-45.21	-45.21

Block 3:

return of funds (on 1st)	100	100										
funds contributed (on 1st)	100	100	100	100	100	100	100	100	100	100	100	100
cumulative own funds contr.	100	200	300	400	500	600	700	800	900	1000	1100	1200
loaned funds												-100
interest (lost)/earned ea month·	-0.85	-1.53	-2.55	-3.29	-4.25	-4.93	-5.95	-6.79	-7.40	-8.49	-9.04	-0.85
cumulative interest		-2.38	-4.93	-8.22	-12.47	-17.40	-23.34	-30.14	-37.53	-46.03	-55.07	-55.92

TABLE 6.6   *Interest Earned/Lost in Sousou*

Month funds returned ($1,200)	cumulative interest earned/(lost) ($)
January	$54.74
February	$44.55
March	$35.34
April	$25.15
May	$15.29
June	$ 5.10
July	($ 4.77)
August	($14.96)
September	($25.15)
October	($35.26)
November	($45.21)
December	($55.92)

NOTES

1. A similar credit association with the same name but with a different spelling ('susu') is reported by Herskovits (1947) in Trinidad. A few studies are now available on the functioning of rotating credit associations in the Dominican Republic (Norvell and Wehrly, 1969); Haiti (Laguerre, 1982); and Jamaica (Katzin, 1959).
2. Rotating credit associations are not peculiar to Martinique or to the Caribbean. They are found all over the world and they function in much the same way (see Wu, 1974; Light, 1972; and Ardener, 1964).

7 Immigrant Households as Overseas Subsidiaries

In a study of urban poverty it is essential to examine the situation of the low-income immigrants, an increasingly important facet of city life, and to ask whether the immigrant experience differs from that of the 'mainstream' urban poor. Poverty is reproduced by the very conditions of immigration. These are people who left their country with little money in search of a better life, and who must now adapt to the structural constraints of the new milieu. Those who find themselves in a negative migration category, as illegal or undocumented aliens, will be further hindered in their flight from poverty. The immigration status by itself is not the determining factor, however, since some immigrants in the negative group are able to overcome that burden and eventually do well in their newly-adopted country. It becomes an obstacle when other factors are added, such as, for example, the inability to acquire permanent resident status and to find a good job. In our attempt to understand the process by which poverty is reproduced in urban Martinique it is crucial to pay attention to that negative category of immigrants because of their relatively large numbers in the slums and squatter settlements of Fort-de-France.[1]

In the previous chapters we have spoken of the family household as a multiproduct firm. As multiproduct firms develop multinational operations, so does the Caribbean family. To circumvent poverty, it may develop foreign subsidiaries. A study of immigrants is central in enlarging our understanding of the multinationalisation of the family as an economic corporation.

By and large, firms have become multinational entities in order to make larger profits and expand their revenues by developing subsidiaries, exploiting foreign markets, diversifying their products, decentralising management, and reducing the risks of bankruptcy. They are able to accomplish those goals chiefly because of favourable conditions abroad, in terms of tax incentives and the monetary and fiscal policies of the host government. Through international migration, the family, too, is divided into headquarters at home and subsidiary households abroad, which hope to accomplish similar goals.

The family headquarters first manages to help one of its members to migrate to a foreign land to operate as a subsidiary. The purposes of the subsidiary are to strengthen its own position abroad (that is to get legal immigrant status, find a job, purchase a house) in order to help the members left behind (that is, to send remittances, to help others to migrate); to serve as a way-station for incoming relatives (welcoming them and helping them adjust to the new society), and, as the headquarters declines, to be responsible for the well-being of its members.

We cannot understand the problems of adaptation faced by immigrants without paying attention to the not so obvious connections with conditions of the homeland. The immigrant develops a budget by taking into consideration the welfare of the family left behind. The money that he or she makes is not used entirely to care for the immediate household: some of it is sent back home. The immigrant does not even control the expenses of the immediate household because parents left behind may send relatives or friends to stay for a while until they are able to find employment and move to their own quarters.

For the family headquarters in St Lucia, Dominica, or Haiti, sending a member to Martinique is a long-term investment. It is a family decision in effect, that investing abroad will be more productive than investing at home. Both the headquarters and the subsidiary are expected to help the other and to make a profit. The success of the headquarters, however, in many instances depends on the success of the subsidiary.

GENERAL PROFILE OF THE IMMIGRANT POPULATION

The immigrant population is heavily concentrated in Lower Sainte Thérèse, especially in the Canal Alaric and Ravine Moreau sections of the neighbourhood. There are also immigrants in the squatter settlements such as Volga Plage. Although they make up only 1.3 per cent of the entire population of Fort-de-France, immigrants represent close to 7.8 per cent of Lower Sainte Thérèse (ADUAM 1984, p. 1). They are more numerous there than in the other slums and squatter settlements of the city because of the proximity of Lower Sainte Thérèse to the port of embarkation and disembarkation and the business district, and also because it is a bit easier to find cheap rentals here than elsewhere in the city.

In terms of their legal status the immigrants do not form a homogeneous community. Some are permanent residents, others are illegal aliens, and others are 'commuting' immigrants. Many itinerant vendors are in this last category. These are individuals who purchase dry goods from their 'home' islands, or from Puerto Rico, Curaçao, or the United States, and commute to Martinique to sell their merchandise. Several Haitian *madan sara* (retailers) belong to that group.

According to ADUAM 13 per cent of the housing available in the Lower Sainte Thérèse neighbourhood was rented to immigrants (ADUAM, 1984, p. 2). The rate of unemployment in the immigrant groups was calculated to be approximately 14 per cent. Among the active population 33.8 per cent worked for the port, 25 per cent were housekeepers and 27.7 per cent were self-employed (as tailors, vendors, and so on) (ADUAM, 1984, p. 5). Family revenues were found to be very modest: 72.6 per cent were below the threshold of poverty as defined by the government, 17.6 per cent earned between 3000 and 5000 francs per month; 3.2 per cent between 5000 and 7000 francs; and 5.9 per cent earned a very irregular monthly income, which could not be computed with any precision (ADUAM, 1984, p. 6).

CASE HISTORIES

A good way to present the data on the immigrant groups, in order to show the mechanisms by which poverty is reproduced, is to set out individual case histories. These offer concrete representations of the many problems newcomers face in their adaptation to city life. In case histories we can observe similarities and differences between immigrants as they become integrated into the city. We shall examine the specificity of the Haitian case, for example, in relation to the experiences of the St Lucian and Dominican immigrants, and gain general ideas about the daily reproduction of poverty among these three groups.

Case 1: A St Lucian Household

The first case is the household headed by a woman named Catherine from St Lucia in Volga Plage, a squatter settlement of Fort-de-France. Born in 1939 Catherine emigrated from St Lucia to Martinique in 1949. Her mother let her join her father here in the hope that once she began working, Catherine would send her some money. If not for that prospect, the mother would not have allowed her to leave St Lucia.

After she migrated to Martinique, Catherine completed her elementary education, then worked in the city as a domestic servant.

Catherine's husband was also from St Lucia and worked as a docker. He did not support her financially on a continuing basis, although they have seven children together. The husband supported the wife and children he had left in St Lucia – that was his reason for making money in Martinique. Now they are divorced and the husband has returned to live in St Lucia. After Catherine's eldest daughter completed high school she earned a diploma in steno–dactylography, then went also to live and work in St Lucia. The six younger children live with Catherine in a crowded one-bedroom house that she owns in Volga Plage.

The economy of the household is maintained by the monthly allowance the mother receives for her children from the French government and by the 1580 francs she earns monthly as a domestic servant. Notwithstanding these economic conditions Catherine continued for many years to send remittances to St Lucia to her old mother, sometimes taking a bite from the government allowances for that purpose. This is a case of a household in permanent crisis. More than thirty years after migrating to Martinique the woman's economic situation has not improved at all. Her husband's inability to help and the size of the family have turned her situation from bad to worse.

In this example a subsidiary household is feeding financially two headquarters households. Part of the money earned by the subsidiary was sent to the wife's mother and part to the husband's first wife in St Lucia. The problem confronted by the subsidiary was not a lack of income, but rather the fact that the money was channelled to extraterritorial households. Poverty was reproduced daily here because this immigrant household, while supporting a man and enabling him to earn a salary, did not have access to his total revenue. The example indicates that the total revenues of the household may not necessarily be used to solve the immediate problems of the household.

Catherine's case is representative of the plight of the larger St Lucian immigrant population in Fort-de-France. The majority of them live in Lower Sainte Thérèse (Canal Alaric and Ravine Moreau) and Volga Plage. In the ADUAM and INSEE surveys individuals from St Lucia form the largest group of immigrants in these two sections of the Lower Sainte Thérèse neighbourhood. They form all in all thirty-one separate households (ADUAM, 1984; INSEE unpublished).

In the ADUAM and INSEE surveys we find that 48.39 per cent of the households consisted of only one person; 9.68 per cent of the households were headed by women. In 19.35 per cent of the households both the husband and the wife were born in St Lucia. In 19.35 per cent of the households the husband was Martinican and the wife St Lucian; and in 3.22 per cent of the households the husband was St Lucian and the wife Martinican. Additionally, in 19.35 per cent of the households, there were additional kin or friends (brother-in-law, godchild, sister-in-law, grandchild, mother-in-law). Only six children under sixteen years old were found (ADUAM, 1984; INSEE, unpublished).

The median income for the St Lucian population was estimated at 1500 francs per month. Twenty-two (40.74 per cent) of the adults were unemployed. As for the occupational status of this immigrant population, 14 per cent were unskilled workers, 28 per cent were masons, 44 per cent domestic servants, and 24 per cent street vendors (ADUAM, 1984; INSEE, unpublished).

Case 2: A Haitian Household

The second case concerns a Haitian couple who have been living in Sainte Thérèse for seven years. They settled first in the Canal Alaric zone, but now live in the upper side of the Sainte Thérèse parish in the midst of a large middle-class population. Anthony, the head of the household, was born in 1940 in Haiti, completed his elementary schooling there, and emigrated to Martinique in 1978. By profession he is a mason, and has been doing independent construction work in Fort-de-France for homeowners who call on him from time to time.

The woman, Solange, who lives with Anthony was also born in Haiti, in 1940. They met in Fort-de-France, fell in love, and decided to rent an apartment together. Their legal status was ambiguous and they did not want to talk much about it. However, they did mention that they came by plane directly from Port-au-Prince. The woman was unemployed at the time of the interview. Like Anthony she had the equivalent of an elementary education.

The couple shares the apartment with a friend, Rosita. She was given Anthony's address by his mother in Haiti, who arranged for her to be her son's guest until she was able to be on her own. She was born in Haiti, was single, had completed elementary school, and had recently migrated to the city. She was also unemployed and supported financially by Anthony, the only breadwinner of the household.

The apartment has a living room, a bedroom, and a kitchen. Rosita was sleeping in the living room at the time of the interview. In addition there is a shower with running water outside the house. The monthly rent is 500 francs, and utilities amount to an extra monthly fee of 16 francs for water, 75 francs for electricity, and 70 francs for gas. All in all they pay 661 francs each month just for shelter, or what we might call overheads.

I have registered the expenses of the household for a seven day period in order to show how tightly they must keep their budget to make ends meet (see Table 7.1).

TABLE 7.1   *A Week of Household Expenses (July 1985)*

Items	Cost (fr)	Place
Rice	84	Supermarket
Bus transportation	6.40	—
Meat (beef)	20	Butcher shop
Cake	11	Supermarket
Doctor's Visit	95	—
Blood Analysis	58.05	—
Bus transportation	3.20	—
Water Cress	3.00	Public Market
Vegetable	6.00	Retail Shop
Potatoes	1.50	Retail Shop
Squash	6.00	Public Market
Paté	3.50	Retail Shop
Meat	19.20	Butcher Shop
Half a bread	2.05	Retail Shop
Meat	35.00	Butcher Market
Red Beans	45.00	Public Market
Plantain	7.00	Public Market
Potatoes	6.00	Public Market
Medicine	6.50	Public Market
Yam	14.00	Public Market
Half a Bread	2.05	Retail Shop
Milk	3.50	Retail Shop
Coffee	2.50	Retail Shop

The expenses for the week amount to 564 francs. Anthony, the only working person in the household, averages monthly wages of 2500 francs. Even though they are not likely to incur medical expenses every month, the ordinary expenses of the household come close to 2256 francs per month, excluding remittances sent home (approximately 250 francs), but including the wife's fare and meals bought outside the house. On top of this are the 661 francs used for the monthly rent and utilities. This breakdown of household expenditures allows us to understand the day-to-day existence of the poor and how money goes from hand to mouth with little possibility for saving. In this case the live-in friend drains the little money this couple could accumulate for savings.

This household is, in fact, on the verge of crisis. Unless the two women are able to find employment or receive some financial help from the government, the household economy will remain in a difficult position. If the man is unable to continue to produce for any reason an income of at least 2500 francs, the household would simply be unable to support itself.

This case is symptomatic of the process of adaptation of low-income Haitian immigrants in Fort-de-France. A sample of twenty-two households from the ADUAM and INSEE surveys was selected for further analysis. These households are located in Volga Plage and Sainte Thérèse, and comprise a total of thirty-eight people.

Women were heads of households in 18.18 per cent of the sample. These households consisted of a mother and her children. None of them were receiving family allowances or social security from the French government. In all instances the mother worked to sustain herself and her children.

In 9.09 per cent of the households Haitian women were living with Martinican men and in another 18.18 per cent of Haitian women were living with Haitian men to whom they were not married. In only 4.54 per cent of the sample were Haitian men living with the Martinican woman. With one exception the Haitian men met their wives or women they live with in Martinique.

Half of the cases consisted of migrants who were living either by themselves (22.73 per cent) or with a relative or friend from Haiti (27.27 per cent). This latter strategy helps a recent migrant or family member from Haiti feel at home in the early phase of the resettlement process, and also sometimes saves the newcomer money.

The median income for employed Haitians was estimated at 1900 francs per month. Only 16 per cent were unemployed. By occupation 16 per cent were dressmakers, 20 per cent domestic servants, 16 per cent unskilled workers, 28 per cent masons, 4 per cent tailors. The professions or skills of the unemployed (16 per cent) are not known. All the Haitian immigrants who were living in Sainte Thérèse and Volga Plage in 1985 came to Martinique in or after 1977 (ADUAM, 1984; INSEE, unpublished).

The situation of the Haitian immigrant shows an extra item in the budget constraints of the household in addition to the remittances factor. From an economic standpoint the friend in the house plays a parasitic role. She is financially supported by the breadwinner, and her presence wipes out any possibility of saving by the rest of the household. Daily reproduction of poverty in that immigrant household is structurally linked to the additional burden. The family ends up bearing the cost, which otherwise would be picked up by the state.

Case 3: A Dominican Household

Through the ADUAM and INSEE surveys we were able to identify seven immigrants from Dominica who were living in Sainte Thérèse and Volga Plage. Only one case was found where both husband and wife were from Dominica. In three cases the husband was either from Martinique or St Lucia.

In this group we find a mechanic, three domestic servants, and an itinerant vendor. The Dominicans migrated to Martinique in or after 1974. Their median income is estimated at 1200 francs per month. One adult was unemployed (ADUAM, 1984; INSEE, unpublished).

The following case gives a glimpse of the experience of the Dominicans in Fort-de-France. This is a couple in which the husband is Martinican and the wife is from Dominica. They live in Volga Plage, a squatter settlement in Fort-de-France. The husband was born in 1931, has the equivalent of an elementary school education, and is a fisherman by trade. His wife was born in Dominica in 1958 and migrated to Martinique in 1974. The man is much older than his wife, but makes enough money to support his family financially. The wife had completed her high school education and has had secretarial training, earning a diploma in shorthand and typing while she was still living in Dominica. She was allowed to migrate so that she could take care of herself and her parents. Every now and then she sends her parents remittances.

Before marrying his wife the man had five children from two previous women: two with another Dominican woman and three with a Martinican woman. He has now two more children with his Dominican wife. Because the man is a fisherman, he was able to keep a family on both islands. Now he seems to be devoted almost exclusively to his second Dominican wife. Now when he goes fishing, his wife helps sell the catch.

Over the years he has been able to send his children to school and to build a three-bedroom house with running water, electricity, a bathroom, and such major appliances as a refrigerator-freezer and a washing machine. The house stands on state-owned land and was built with the help of friends and neighbours who served as carpenters, masons, and electricians. Thus he did not have to pay for labour, but solely for the materials. Through all his tribulations in Martinique he has continued to send money for his mother and younger sisters still living in Dominica.

Since the wife does not have a steady job apart from her husband's venture, the economy of the household rests on the ability of the husband to catch enough fish both to sell in the public market and to feed his family. This is a case of the large family that depends on the husband's fishing skills for its survival. Despite a façade of contentment, the family undergoes great stress to make ends meet.

This final case indicates that headquarters households, because they depend on subsidiaries for their existence, must be taken into consideration in an analysis of immigrant household budgets. Although the money sent home is usually little, at times large sums are also requested, especially when there is illness or death in the original household. When employment is available, an immigrant may work two jobs so as to be able to help family members left behind. That is rarely a possibility in Martinique, and remittances can therefore have a very negative impact on the operating budget of the immigrant household.

ETHNICITY

The question of the reproduction of poverty among the poor St Lucian, Haitian, and Dominican immigrants must be framed also within the context of ethnicity. Ethnicity is important on two grounds to an understanding of their adaptation to the city. On the one hand, the mainstream residents have a number of confused perceptions of the immigrants, and on the other, the immigrants are aware of these negative views. By and large, the poor immigrants are seen in an unfavourable, stereotypical way by the larger community. For example, the Dominicans and St Lucians are referred to as 'anglais' (the British people) in contrast to the Martinicans who consider themselves as 'français' (French men and women). The former are believed to be engaged in the drug and contraband business. Although the majority of these immigrants are law-abiding people, the Martinicans who do not know them on a personal level have developed negative perceptions of the Afro-Anglo group because once in a while one of their number is caught by the police, and these occurrences are reported in the newspapers and on television and radio.

France-Antilles, the major daily newspaper in the French Caribbean headquartered in Martinique, reported in its edition of 1 October 1979 that the current trend in banditism in the French Islands started with the illegal immigration of Dominicans leaving their own island territory in search of an easy life. On the other hand, Haitian immigrants are perceived by the larger population as illiterate but honest and hard-working people. Progressive sectors in Martinican society have shown some interest in the plight of Haitian refugees and have helped them on some occasions.

We find here the phenomenon of 'reconstituted ethnicity'. Ethnicity is not unvariant. It is 'constituted' and so can be 'reconstituted'. It is developed by an ethnic group's circumstances including the cultural and social reality lived by the immigrant group, and the perceptions of outsiders as well. Awareness of one's ethnicity as a member of a majority group at home will take another shape abroad, when one happens to be relegated to a minority group status. St Lucian ethnicity at home, where these immigrants belong to a majority group, is not the same as St Lucian ethnicity in Martinique because they belong to a minority group. In Martinique their ethnicity is reconstituted by the very fact that the group is relegated to a minority and dependent status; that is, in economic and political terms, they are not considered equal, much less superior, to the members of the majority community. The term 'reconstitution' of ethnicity implies that some elements of national culture are being adapted to new circumstances. Within each ethnic group questions of class influence the constitution of one's ethnicity. The immigrants are no exception to that principle. However, a comparative analysis of ethnicity and class cannot be carried out here, because the majority of the immigrants in our sample belong to the lower-class.

The three case histories show characteristic ways immigrants arrange their lives. They devise strategies of adaptation that seem to be in line with their own cultural backgrounds. At the same time they do things they might not have done, or would have done differently, if they were still at home.

Ethnicity is the single element that pulls members of the group together and underlines their desire to help one another. Immigrants with no shelter join those who have a place. The immigrant community itself is a shelter: the place where one withdraws to revitalise one's energy and recoup one's strengths.

In the process of reconstituting their ethnicity people use various strategies to adapt to the new environment. For some their persistent strengths depend on their persistent identification with the community. This may explain why many prefer to marry someone from the same ethnic group. Others prefer to assimilate directly to mainstream culture by marrying someone from the majority group, a strategy that may be used as a way of legalising their status.

The immigrants reconsruct their ethnicity consciously or unconsciously to meet new challenges, to respond to constraints from the larger system, and to articulate their actions, views and goals to the new reality. The notion of the reconstitution of ethnicity implies that the content of ethnicity varies as one migrates from one's national territory to another country. In the situation of migration ethnicity may also vary over time because of the arrangement and evolutionary position of some groups in society. The perception of the mainstream *vis-à-vis* the group varies as well. For example, although Haitian refugees are seen as lower-class individuals, the local perception of the group has changed as the result of the influence of Haitian music in Martinique. The invasion of Haitian music and musicians has been seen as an obstacle to the development of the truly Martinican music. Haitian musicians are believed to have made a bundle in Martinique in the past two decades. Haitian artists are consequently seen as cultural imperialists, imposing their musical genres and influencing Martinicans' musical taste (see Hurbon, 1983, p. 1993).

The process by which ethnicity is reconstituted must be seen as part of the adaptation of the immigrants to their adopted land. It is a form of integration, a way of overcoming obstacles that could contribute to the reproduction of poverty among the immigrants. It is the result of both endogenous and exogenous influences.

IMMIGRANTS AND POVERTY

A number of observations can be made about the adaptation of the immigrants to the city of Fort-de-France. The St Lucians form the oldest and largest group of foreign immigrants, followed by the Haitians and then by the Dominicans. Only one case was reported in which an emigrant went first to England and then to Martinique. The majority migrated directly from the sending to the receiving community.

What we encounter in Fort-de-France is the migration, not of peasants, but of urban dwellers. The majority of the immigrants had lived in a city before coming to Martinique. They have skills that are marketable in the urban setting.

While the majority of the migrants tend to marry people of their native group, there is a marked trend to intergroup marriage, especially of migrants with Martinicans. This trend will probably be even more pronounced in the second generation. For those without a legal status, there is some advantage in intermarriage, which allows them an opportunity to become permanent residents or citizens.

The other pronounced trend is the way in which the newcomers share apartment life with kin and friends. This pattern is likely to hold through the process of adapting, until the newcomers are able to find jobs and move out. In any case such an arrangement can only be temporary, because the hosts seldom have extra rooms and they must share their own quarters with their guests.

Because they lack financial means, the immigrants start living in the poorest zones of the city where they can find cheap housing or live with friends who have preceded them. The arrival of new immigrants spatially reinforces the class division of Martinican society. The newcoming poor simply join a lower-class neighbourhood.

The immediate neighbours of the immigrants are also urban dwellers and mostly migrants from the rural zones. The migrants are not welcomed to the city as first class citizens, for they are introduced into an area that is as poor or poorer than that they left behind. Through these neighbours they receive their first feedback about the city; neighbours also help them find jobs and decipher the social environment.

The immigrants live in a ghetto-like environment with dilapidated housing, often without bathrooms – and they end up being limited to the perspective of their poor neighbours. Thus they are unable to develop contacts with people who could help them to achieve upward mobility.

The financial support migrants give to friends and family members at home and abroad takes a big bite from their already ragged household economies. These payments are a constant source of stress because of the fragmentation of the extended family in different lands.

Since migrants are mostly from the lower-class, we may speak of class homogeneity among them. The lower-class migrants live in both the squatter settlements and the slums of Fort-de-France. Migrant households support the merchants who travel back and forth between Martinique and their homelands. Among the migrants the merchants find places to stay, and in some instances business partners as well.

This commuting population furnishes a continuous supply of news for the island residents about the most recent events, local commentaries ('*zin*'), and the degrading living conditions of their respective islands. The commuting migrants serve as a cultural link between the migrant community and the homeland, and they also find among the immigrants a ready-made market for their goods.

Because they work as itinerant traders, the presence of Haitian market women is more visible than that of other immigrants in the business district.[2] The street vendors, in sharp competition with the local retailers, display their merchandise along certain streets such as the Boulevard General de Gaulle. They are recognised by the local population through the style of their dress, their hairdos, and the form of creole they speak.

The street vendors and itinerants are often extensions or local representatives of the commuting merchants. Their activity is a form of self-employment in the informal sector outside the mainstream economy; they are not dependent on Martinican employers.

The presence of Dominican, St Lucian, and Haitian immigrants is made known to the larger population also by a small group of prostitutes headquartered on the Route des Religieuses. The women emerge every evening at sundown, ready for business; as the night progresses, they also occupy the area around the Catholic Cathedral in the downtown.

The exploitation of the immigrants is a cause of the reproduction of poverty among them. The migrants are exploited both by their landlords and in the workplace. The macrosystem of capitalist accumulation finds its microexpression in the slum. This fact can be shown through an analysis of slum housing. Many individuals who are long-time residents have built a second home or added on a few rooms to rent to newcomers. Some migrants find themselves renting from a neighbour landlord. The rent per unit is often high, and frequently the unit is not equipped with a kitchen or bathroom. Renting out is one avenue used by slum dwellers to accumulate capital, but to do so they must exploit poor neighbours.

Another area in which the migrants are exploited is in the workplace. They are paid wages lower than that offered the natives for equal work. Many are engaged as day or week labourers with no employment security and no fringe benefits. Since they are often paid lower-than-minimum wages, local employers are glad to employ them to save money and maximise profit. The migrants are very vulnerable, since they must accept whatever an unscrupulous employer offers them.

REPRODUCTION OF POVERTY

The reproduction of poverty in the households of migrants, despite their efforts to reconstitute ethnicity, is conditioned by both internal and external structural factors. Migrants face obstacles of three types. First is the external constraint of the legal category in which they are placed by the state. They are not officially welcomed by the state; their presence is barely tolerated, because they are perceived as a burden rather than as potential contributors to society. Martinique being a French territory, the same rules for the immigration of blacks to metropolitan France are applied to the island. They are categorised as unskilled workers. The first months or year in the new country can result in debilitating psychological trauma when migrants cannot obtain a work permit or are given permits with the knowledge that they must be renewed. Migrants are aware that the renewal of their permits – and thus the length of their stays – depends on fluctuations in the economy and on other political factors as well. They have heard stories of the actual deportation of some migrants to their homelands, and they worry about their own chances of staying in their country of adoption. Instead of welcoming and helping the migrant, the state has become an obstacle to the migrant's adaptation and undermines his or her ability to break the cycle of poverty.

Foreigners without an adequate visa are vulnerable in their interaction with the larger population. There is always the threat that someone can report them for any reason to the immigration office. This fear has forced some, especially the Haitians, to remain quiet and 'mind their own business', and it prevents them from fighting for their rights, especially when dealing with unfair employers. Fear of deportation thus also helps reproduce poverty among the immigrants.

A second external obstacle is the attitudes of the population toward the foreign immigrant. Generally speaking they are looked down on because they are poor. This is a vicious circle: because they are neither citizens nor permanent residents, they cannot benefit from state allowances, social security, or unemployment benefits. Immigrants thus find themselves in a category below that of the ordinary Martinican urban dwellers. For that matter immigrants who are not considered by the state as permanent residents cannot be compared with citizens. The Martinican who loses his job can fall back on his social security benefits. The illegal migrant cannot. The non-resident foreigner is in fact a resident migrant, but is not considered as such by the law.

Still another problem is the inability of immigrants to operate in the system. They would be in a better position to deal with the first two obstacles if they had not brought with them an internal obstacle that hinders their adaptation. Migrants must often send remittances home or may take on dependents to live with them, which deepens their own problems. Theoretically the presence of a parent or a friend could be a blessing, pulling resources together, helping to pay the rent, but in practice it complicates matters and may become more onerous than living alone. We can imagine the employed migrant feeling compelled to pay for an unemployed friend and thereby made unable to take care of his own or his family's problems.

The notion of reconstituted ethnicity sheds its own light on the mechanisms of the reproduction of poverty among the poor immigrants of Fort-de-France. Examining the changes the immigrant's self-image undergoes leads us to look at the reactions of the state and the larger mainstream community to the immigrants, and especially the obstacles placed in their way. In the daily struggle against poverty the immigrants continually make personal and cultural responses to the structural constraints of the environment. The reproduction of poverty in this segment of Martinican society is made possible in part because of the unstable ethnic identity of the newcomers, although other factors too account for the reproduction of poverty in immigrant households.

The data clearly indicate that first generation immigrant households can be viewed as extensions of family households in the sending society. In the vocabulary of the firm they can fairly be called 'subsidiaries'. The role of subsidiaries is to contribute to their own economic success as well as to that of the headquarters. The immigrants not only worry about the family members left behind, but often help the headquarters household by sending remittances home and by helping other members to migrate.

Remittances have generally been studied in terms of their impact on the local economies in which the recipients live, rather than in terms of their impact on the budgets of immigrant households.[3] Remittances are profit made by the headquarters household from its overseas investment (or subsidiaries). To understand the mechanism of the reproduction of poverty, one must look at how the relationship between the headquarters and the subsidiary affects the subsidiary. Let us chart the impact over five different areas.

First, we notice that part of the subsidiary budget is used to sustain the headquarters, through the regular remittances sent to the parents.

The household cannot rely on that portion to cover household expenditures. This is the first breach in the subsidiary's budget.

Second, we notice that, in addition to remittances, part of the budget is used to defray expenses resulting from the presence of a friend or relative sent by the headquarters to live in the subsidiary household. The subsidiary has no say in this decision, but is still responsible for the expenses.

Third, we see again that short and long-term decisions taken by the subsidiary are affected not only by conditions in the newly-adopted country, but also by circumstances in the home country where the headquarters are. For example, if the breadwinner in the headquarters loses his or her job, the sending family will be even more dependent on the subsidiary. It may be that the breadwinner in the subsidiary must do more than one job to meet the new demand from the headquarters.

Fourth, the subsidiary families may start saving money from their already meagre revenues to pay for the migration of another family member from the headquarters. This money is not used to meet the needs of the subsidiary, but rather those of the headquarters.

Fifth, decisions concerning the future of the subsidiary must take into consideration the future of the headquarters as well. Subsidiary households are aware that with age, old parents will become more dependent on them financially. They may contemplate measures bringing parents to the subsidiary household. If a father dies, the mother may be invited to join the subsidiary household, and this leads to a merger, as discussed earlier in Chapter 3.

If the subsidiary is operating on a tight budget, any one of the five factors mentioned may affect its well-being negatively. Poverty will be reproduced daily unless other measures are taken to offset deficiencies created by the dependency of the headquarters on the subsidiary.

NOTES

1. A feasibility study pertaining to the housing of the immigrants was done by ADUAM (1984b). It concentrates exclusively on two sections of Sainte Thérèse, namely, Canal Alaric and Ravine Moreau. See also Tanic (1985) and Letchimy (1984b).
2. Glondu traces the participation of St Lucian and Haitian vendors in the central public market of Fort-de-France to the early sixties. He notes: 'Il convient toutefois de noter que cette évolution [la spécialisation dans la

distribution de certains produits] a été favorisée par la pénétration de plus en plus importante d'étrangers venant des îles voisines, à partir des années 60. Ils ont introduit sur le marché un certain nombre de marchandises qui n'existent pas sur place et jouent un grand rôle dans l'approvisionnement des marchands d'épices et produits manufacturés du grand marché, faisant régulièrement la navette entre la Martinique et leur île d'origine . . . . Ce sont pour la plupart des Haitiens et des Sainte-Luciens' (Glondu, 1983, p. 17).

3.   For a review of the literature on the impact of remittances in Caribbean societies, see Stinner, de Albuquerque, and Bryce-Laporte (1982).

8 Concluding Remarks

The city of Fort-de-France, Martinique, is used throughout this study as a social laboratory in which to test the hypothesis that urban poverty is reproduced over time. Each chapter examines a substantive element of the general mechanism of social reproduction – for example, the household, the shop, strategy of immigration. When broken down into its components, each element is seen as a pivotal point at which asymmetric relations affect the reproduction of the unit, that is, the family, individual, or enterprise. We come to understand that 'social reproduction' refers, not necessarily to the reproduction of each element, but rather to the reproduction of the identity of the unit.

Social reproduction is not mass reproduction of identical units, because the notion of reproduction contains the ideas both of sameness and difference. Units may be the same in regard to their structural position in the system. They will thus be the same insofar as the social relations from which they emerge reproduce a certain identity. Units will also differ, because social reproduction implies social change. When we talk about the reproduction of poverty, it is understood that the dominant sector of society has not remained the same over time, nor have the poor, and thus the relations of one sector to the other must also have changed. However, these three factors – dominant sector, dominated sector, and asymmetric relation – have maintained their identities with respect to one another.

It is of utmost importance in the analysis of social reproduction of poverty to decompose the poor sector so as to identify the articulation of the components within the sector and as they mesh with the dominant sector. Barel (1972, p. 154) reminds us that we cannot think of the reproduction of a unit in society as an isolated phenomenon. In the present case the reproduction of the dominated sector of society implies the reproduction of the dominant sector and the maintenance of asymmetric relations between both. In other words the reproduction of the system implies the reproduction of the units that make up the system. This rationale leads us to analyse such units as the grocery shop or the rotating credit association. Each is reproduced in its own way, contributing at the same time to the reproduction of the total system.

Throughout this analysis the concept of social reproduction is not used in any restrictive way. In fact, it is seen, in the words of

Bandyopadhyay (1986, p. 192) in terms of 'the maintenance of the structural identity of a social formation through time'. What is reproduced is the asymmetry of social relations.

The reproduction of each unit depends on the reproduction of the total system, and vice versa. Although the relationship of each unit to the total system is vital, the relationship of each unit to every other may be necessary but not essential. The relationship of a unit to another may be 'direct', that is, depending on the other for its existence, or 'indirect', that is, the relationship may be mediated by the total system. The relationship can also be asymmetrical (boutique owner versus poor immigrants) or symmetrical (family versus rotating credit association members).

Social reproduction entails the production of asymmetrical social relations. The reproduction of the system does not mean necessarily that the same agents reproduce themselves over time, but that the asymmetry of class relations remains constant over time. The invariant in the scheme of reproduction is the asymmetry of class relations: individual agents may change their positions in the system. Thus it is possible for any poor slum dweller to move from lower to middle-class. The structural characteristics of the system are not changed by such individual movement.

Reproduction of poverty does not mean only that the poor as individuals reproduce poverty transgenerationally. Some individuals may escape from poverty. Nor do the poor form a homogeneous group; rather they are diversified and stratified, because individual members hold different positions in the subsystem. It is the system that is able to reproduce its own identity, and the reproduction of the structure of asymmetric class relations that breeds inequality. As the structure is reproduced, the same actors or progenitors do not necessarily occupy the same positions. With the passage of time and their own efforts they may achieve some form of upward mobility. However, as Perrson (1978, p. 24) puts it, 'the reproduction of agents to a given set of positions is intimately tied to the reproduction of the social relation itself'. We have seen that where members of the working class do not reproduce themselves, they are replaced by incoming immigrants who do the same job.

As we clarify the issues pertaining to the process of reproduction, it is also important to study the conditions under which a system may fail to reproduce itself, especially in terms of intra- and inter-systemic relations. Godelier (1982, p. 259) speaks of the need to analyse 'the conditions of "reproduction" (and of "non-reproduction") of social systems, taking into account the constraints imposed by their internal structures and their ecological environments'.

A study of social reproduction is implicitly a study of the reproduction of the society or the identity (what we might call social DNA) of the society. However, such was not my ambition here. We have identified certain units and analysed how they are articulated with the larger societal system. These units are reproduced as parts of the marginal zones and the institutions that comprise them. The reproduction of the periphery must be seen as the reproduction of one of the poles that give the system its essential identity.

If we define society as a 'structure of positions', the reproduction of the dominated system is made possible by the reproduction of strategic elements or of the positions they occupy. The maintenance and reproduction of these positions matters more than the people who fill them. These positions are strategic in the sense that they link one sector of society vertically and horizontally to another. They play a mediating role, linking poor neighbourhoods or poor people to extra-community or national institutions – for example, the *boutique* to wholesalers, the *sousou* to the formal banking system, the family to the school system, and the immigrants to the agencies of the state. Inequality is articulated and maintained through those positions.

The reproduction of the slum, when viewed with the division of the working class into a core and a periphery, is a double process. The core corresponds to the individuals who are socially integrated and the periphery to those who are not, such as the first generation immigrants. The working class has a backup system – the immigrant wave – in case there is any decrease in its reproduction.

The study of social reproduction leads to the conclusion that the phenomenon cannot finally be understood without a theory of the state. The reproduction of inequality is part of a larger process, that of the reproduction of the state. Even the study of specific components must be related to a larger theory that explains state reproduction. Martinique, however, is not a state but a Department of France. The policies of the Paris administration, as well as the fluctuation of the *bourse*, necessarily have their repercussions on urban Martinique. The reproduction of the upper class depends largely on the relationships they are able to maintain with the political and commercial establishment of metropolitan France.

In the Martinican situation the reproduction of urban poverty means three basic things: first, the production – since each reproduction is a production – of a reality, that is, asymmetric relations between two poles (see also Barel, 1972); a reality can be visible as well as hidden; second, the production of a space in which the articulation of asymmetric relations finds its infrastructural and superstructural basis of support; and finally the production of a hierarchy of positions and of asymmetric relations within the same pole. Urban poverty is the consequence or the result of a series of unequal exchanges between the employer and the employee, the neighbourhood and the state, the wholesaler and the retailer, and the retailer and the client.

When viewed together with the state, the question of the reproduction of urban poverty seems clearly linked to state policies. It has been argued that the reproduction of urban poverty is partly due to the urban bias of development policies. This is not a phenomenon peculiar to the Caribbean. Development policies tend to favour the capital city more than the rural areas. A major portion of the national budget is usually invested in services and facilities that benefit the capital city directly or indirectly. This bias gives a tremendous importance to the city as the political, administrative, and economic centre of the nation. As a consequence, it is further argued, the country is totally dominated by the urban establishment. As Lipton (1977, p. 68) puts it, 'everywhere it is government by the city, from the city, for the city'. However, foreign donors have recently targeted rural organisations for financial aid. Instead of going to the city bureaucracy, they go directly to the rural people. The Inter-American Foundation is now following this policy in Latin America and the Caribbean. The positive point in this procedure is that the neediest are getting some help, but it also raises fundamental questions about the internal security of the state.

In the light of the explanations we have discovered for mechanisms of the reproduction of poverty, we can ask what responses are provided by the state to solve the same problems. The Caribbean governments have all been concerned in one way or another with finding a solution to urban poverty and have attempted to develop programmes and policies. The degree of their success should be judged against the odds they have faced: small and weak economies, political dependence, internal strife, overpopulation, and inequality in the distribution of wealth.

To respond to the problem of urban poverty, Caribbean governments have developed five main strategies: addressing basic needs, decentralisation, industrialisation by invitation, specific remedial intervention and transfer of money.

Basic Needs Policies

One frequently-stated policy of the Caribbean governments is to meet the basic needs of the urban and rural population.[1] 'Basic needs' means the social environment and institutions geared to the basic well-being of the people, for example, the creation of new jobs, raising the minimum wage, and the maintenance, expansion, and upgrading of schools and hospitals.

The implementation of basic needs programmes however often benefits the middle and upper classes more than the truly poor who are the government's target. The services offered are not necessarily free of charge, and consequently the poor may not have easy access to them.

The politics of basic needs requires for its successful outcome a restructuring of the domestic economies and national priorities. The translation of this policy strategy into action has not always been successful. The sprawling slums and squatter settlements even on the islands with the highest per capita incomes in the region is an indication that much needs to be done to make basic needs programmes more effective.

Industrialisation by Invitation

Another strategy used by Caribbean governments to reduce urban poverty has been to provide incentives to foreign businessmen to operate their manufacturing plants in the capital cities of the islands. In the past three decades Puerto Rico, with 'Operation Bootstrap', has been the showcase for this kind of urban development programme. The reasoning behind this strategy is that these manufacturing plants should provide countless jobs to the unemployed, give a boost to the local economy, and develop a strong link between the local economy and the US economy.

The path of industrialisation by invitation has been followed by Jamaica, for example, in the aftermath of its independence from Britain, and by Haiti during the Jean-Claude Duvalier regime. Although this strategy does provide jobs to the unemployed, it also complicates further the mathematics of Caribbean economics and politics. The foreign-based industries, by and large, produce goods not for the local market but rather for North American and European markets, and they serve to encourage rural to urban migration. As more and more people are leaving the agricultural fields in search of an industrial job in the capital city, a structural problem is created in the economies of the islands.[2] The people end by producing goods they do not need, and those they are in need of, such as foodstuffs, they must import (see Barry *et al.*, 1984).

The presence of those industries is on some islands a source of political corruption. Public employees demand bribes to process company papers. High-level government officials take a bite from the profits made by the corporations in exchange for not harassing those 'foreigners'. In some instances industries have hired individuals into managerial positions on the strength of their contacts with government officials. Black (1986, p. 9) has found in the Dominican Republic that 'a revolving door at the upper levels of company and government administration allowed former company managers to serve in important government posts and former government officials to move into company management'.

To accommodate foreign corporations, Caribbean governments have gone so far as to expropriate the land of the urban residents so that manufacturing plants could be built in the city or its vicinity. Despite their limited economic impact, in terms of producing needed employment or goods for the local community, it is increasingly clear that the industrial plants degrade the environmental quality. Hudson (1980, p. 4) has already observed that 'Kingston Harbour and San Juan's Condado Lagoon are so contaminated with sewage from the surrounding urban development that they are no longer safe for swimming, and fishing has suffered. Moreover, air pollution from some industrial plants is increasingly apparent'.

Transfer of Money

The transfer of money is a way to help the poor and the handicapped on a short or long-term basis. Through the tax mechanism the state intervenes in the market process by taking the money from one segment of society and giving it to another segment.

This mechanism operates in two ways. On the one hand, money is taken from working households and redistributed to non-working households. On the other hand, surplus money is transferred from the middle and upper classes to the poor (see Wayne, 1986, p. 129). The transfer of money is a tangible factor in the reproduction of the working class.

The working class comprises two categories of people: those who have employment and those who do not. The transfer of money through taxation is an additional burden on the employed, because it is money subtracted from their income that otherwise could be saved as capital for the purpose of upward mobility. Transfers are preventive measures, so that the unemployed do not become conscious of their conditions and rise against the exploiters or create more problems for the state. Transfers also reproduce the working class while the unemployed wait to be employed.

This strategy has been crucial in preventing social protest in Martinique. Since departmentalisation, the French government has devised a series of welfare benefit schemes, such as, for example, *l'allocation familiale*. The United States government has been doing the same in Puerto Rico. In the light of the experience of the governments of the industrialised world, the Caribbean states, when they have the means, follow in the same direction. Unfortunately not every government in the Caribbean has such welfare programmes.

Specific Remedial Intervention

This category includes the efforts made by the government to attack specific problems related to poverty. Such efforts do not intend to eradicate the problem of urban poverty *per se*. Their rationale is that when a specific manifestation of urban poverty has become too visible, it is an affront to the rest of the community and repulsive to the incoming tourists, and therefore something must be done about it.

Three forms of remedial intervention have been carried out in the Caribbean: the bulldozing of shacks, the creation of new neighbourhoods, and the renewal or construction of housing for low-income families. As poor people migrate to the city, some have built shacks to meet their housing needs. These are seen particularly in the so-called squatter settlements. Slum dwellers have been evicted and their houses bulldozed by the state in Jamaica, Cuba, Haiti, and Puerto Rico, to name just a few islands (Zandvoort, 1979, p. 172). Sometimes eviction is temporary, while the government can build houses for them.[3] Frequently, however, residents are simply pushed out with no hope of being resettled by, or getting compensation from, the state government.

Another strategy is to renovate neighbourhoods or create new ones, as was the case with New Kingston, in Jamaica, and the Cité Militaire in Port-au-Prince, Haiti. After hurricane Hattie in 1961 the government of Belize built a new neighbourhood, Hattieville, to settle the homeless of Belize City (Everitt, 1985, p, 108). Elsewhere in the

Caribbean, new neighbourhoods have been built by the government for the purpose of resettling a sector of society. The buildings are new and the neighbourhoods are the result of much advance planning, so that they tend to have modern structures with all the facilities. Renovation, which is more common, is the process by which the government intervenes in certain neighbourhoods to draw them into the 'orbit of operational space' (Santos, 1979, p. 7) by providing the people with electricity, sewage, running water, and so on.

The third alternative is to develop housing for low-income residents without necessarily altering the conditions in the neighbourhood.[4] The various HLM (*Habitats à loyer modique*) built in Martinique and Guadeloupe by the French government intend to fill that need (Goudet, 1973; Paquette, 1969; Vaugirard, 1985). These are apartment houses built for poor families. At least that was the intention; the result is different. The HLM are seen by leftist Martinicans as a way of keeping the labour reserve quietly at hand to be exploited by capital when they are needed.

The 'projects' often end by being exercises in social engineering, because the state does not take individual preference and kinship organisation into consideration in assigning apartments to families. The main thrust of the state is to provide housing to nuclear families, not to extended families. In cities where residence is organised to accommodate kinship groups, the establishment of housing projects breaks up the spatial proximity of family members to one another.

Bryce-Laporte (1968, p. 533) studied 'urban relocation' and 'public housing' as ways of solving the housing problem in the slums of San Juan, Puerto Rico. He addresses the inability of the urban policy-makers to consider or design for the extended family patterns of the poor, rather than simply developing programmes for urban development. One of the issues is that urban relocation implies uprooting a population from its familiar habitat, however poor that habitat may be, and moving it to government housing. Although these housing schemes may solve the problem of congestion, they create new problems for the cohesion of the extended family and impose new norms in the daily lives of the residents, in that they must follow new rules and adopt new behaviours. The people thus relocated would generally rather stay in their communities, provided the government helps them to refurbish their homes.

Another problem inherent in the housing schemes stems from the reality of political context. Housing units are distributed not to the neediest but to those involved in patron-client relationships. The distribution mechanism is highly politicised.[5] Units are given to those who have supported the party in office, with the help of the local brokers who have interceded on their behalf. Inequality is thus built into the distribution process. The patronage system ensures that those who benefit the most are not the poor, but rather the middle class. The really poor may be prevented from getting housing this way because they cannot pay the monthly rent.

Decentralisation

The third strategy developed to confront the existence of poverty is decentralisation. The rationale here is that centralisation draws the rural population to the city to seek work in the industries there, and the city then becomes the locus of all political and economic power.

In the political science literature decentralisation has come to mean both administrative and political. Spiegel and Walling (1974, p. 5) note that 'administrative decentralization usually refers to the delegation of some managerial functions from a central authority to its lower echelons, its field offices or to a wider circle of functionaries within its institutional framework . . . . Political decentralization, on the other hand, usually refers to sharing, granting, surrendering, or otherwise establishing power to actors (individual or institution) outside its usual institutional framework or jurisdiction.'

The Castro government has employed the decentralisation strategy to reduce the importance of Havana, by building new agricultural and industrial towns. According to Acosta and Hardoy (1973, p. 7) between 1959 and 1962, eighty-three new towns were built in Cuba. Some small cities were helped to develop into larger ones, filling new roles as regional capitals. One such is Nuevitas, which has become an industrial city and a major regional port (Acosta and Hardoy, 1973, p. 42). The administrative decentralisation of Havana was a factor in the decrease in the growth of its population.

The Cuban experience of urbanisation in the context of a socialist state consists of transforming the capital from a parasite metropolis that sucks the lifeblood of the hinterland to a centre of production and services responding to the urban proletariat and the rural areas. It has meant the development of policies detrimental to the interests of the élites, but attuned to the interests of the proletariat. The urban space has been reorganised to meet the imperatives of the revolution.[6] By its own transformation the city has been forced to participate in the revolution.

The government of Barbados has also been pursuing a policy of decentralisation with a view to establishing a hierarchy of urban settlements throughout the island, emphasising regional urban centres, district centres, and village centres (see Potter, 1983, p. 6). In hopes of reducing congestion at Bridgetown, industrial parks were to be established in various parishes. This decentralisation is supposed to produce new jobs for the residents of these parishes, to reduce the rate of unemployment in the rural areas, and to keep rural-to-urban migration at a low level (Potter, 1981, p. 226).

The government of Jamaica has been heading toward a strategy similar to the urban deconcentration proposed in Barbados. The National Physical Plan of 1971 for Jamaica calls for the development of regional centres, subregional centres, and district towns (Hudson, 1980, p. 8). In Trinidad urban planners have proposed the development of 'petro-poles' that would become centres of population and economic growth. The lifeblood of these centres will be sustained by the petroleum industries, which will provide necessary jobs to the residents (Hudson, 1980, p. 10).

The government of the Dominican Republic has attempted to ease the congestion of the city of Santo Domingo by providing incentives to industries that locate outside the city. Except for such industries as Falconbridge's ferronickel plant, Alcoa's bauxite mine, and those involved in the production of sugar, which must by necessity be near the sources of their raw materials, most industrial plants that remain in the city do so because of the services and facilities it offers (Orlando Haza, 1972, p. 50).

In the Caribbean generally decentralisation is to be viewed more as administrative than political. The policy of decentralisation that most of the governments try to follow contains a germ of contradiction. Decentralisation does not mean for them de-emphasising the importance of the capital as a power base (see also Franger, 1978). The struggle for political power is carried on in the urban arena, not in the countryside. Decentralisation means rather stabilising the service sector, reducing population growth, and moving manufacturing to the countryside. Since the capital houses the active voters and is the place where disparities between the rich and the poor are most visible, there are pressures from all sectors to do something for residents of the town. Because the presence of the poor is unpleasant, urban policies are developed directly or indirectly to deal with them.[7]

Another way in which decentralisation has been implemented is in the transfer of the capital to another site, while the former capital remains the economic centre of the country. This was the strategy followed in Belize. In order to ease the crowding in Belize City, Belmopan was created as the new political and administrative centre. Belize City, however, continues to grow, despite the existence of Belmopan, which is little more than a government town (Kearns, 1973).

The various schemes developed by Caribbean governments to deal with the question of urban poverty do not attack the root causes of poverty and inequality, but simply attempt to provide some relief to urban dwellers. Their intention is never to eradicate poverty altogether on the islands. By alleviating the immediate burden of the city dwellers, state policies contribute in some measure to the reproduction of inequality in society and consequently to the reproduction of urban poverty. The Martinican experience is not unique in the region. To the extent that Martinique allows us to understand some of the basic mechanisms of the reproduction of urban poverty, it sheds light on the similar conditions and disparities that exist in the Caribbean in particular and in the Third World in general.

NOTES

1.   For an elaboration and discussion of the issue of basic human needs, especially in the context of urban poverty in Africa, see Sandbrook (1982).
2.   On the impact of industrialisation on agricultural productivity in Puerto Rico, see Safa (1974, p. 21). See also Clarke (1975), Cross (1979), Thomas (1988) and Hope (1986) for the Commonwealth Caribbean.
3.   Butterworth (1980, p. 20) reports such a case in revolutionary Cuba.
4.   On solutions proposed for the construction of low-cost housing for the urban poor in the Caribbean, see, for example, Chin (1978).
5.   Corruption in Martinican politics is briefly discussed in Miles (1986, pp. 75–6).
6.   Cuban urban policies, and especially the role of the microbrigades in the construction of housing for the poor, have been documented and analysed in Eckstein (1977b) and Gugler (1980).
7.   Caribbean urban policies are increasingly influenced by lending institutions such as IMF and the World Bank, which produces its own recommendations (see, for example, World Bank, 1983).

Bibliography

Achéen, René (1983) Pour une Grammaire de L'Histoire Antillaise: 1635–1946, *Les Temps Modernes*, 39 (441–2) Avril–Mai: pp. 1815–35.

Acosta, M. and Hardoy, J. E. (1973) *Urban Reform in Revolutionary Cuba*, Occasional Papers, No. 1 (New Haven: Yale University).

ADUAM (Association Départementale Pour les Etudes d'Urbanisme et D'Aménagement de la Martinique) (1980) *La zône des 50 pas géométriques* (Fort-de-France: ADUAM).

ADUAM (1984a) *La Population Immigrée* (Fort-de-France: ADUAM).

ADUAM (1984b) Ville de Fort-de-France. *Canal Alaric – Ravine Moreau. Etude Préalable. Diagnostic Social.* (Fort-de-France: ADUAM.)

Allen, Vernon L. (1970) *Psychological Factors in Poverty* (Chicago: Markham Publishing Co.).

Anon. (1970) La 'Cour Fruit à Pain', *Bulletin Municipal de Fort-de-France*, Nouvelle Série No. 5 (Mars) p. 43.

Ardener, Shirley (1964) 'The Comparative Study of Rotating Credit Associations', *Journal of the Royal Anthropological Institute*, pp. 94, 201–9.

Armstrong, M. Jocelyn (1985) *Female Domestics in Industrializing Malaysia.* Paper presented to the American Ethnological Association symposium on 'Domestic Workers' at the annual meetings of the American Anthropological Association, Washington DC, December.

Bandyopadhyay, Pradeep (1986) 'Theoretical Approaches to the State and Social Reproduction', in James Dickinson and Bob Russell (eds), *Family, Economy and State: The Social Reproduction Process under Capitalism* (London: Croom Helm).

Barel, Yves (1972) *La Reproduction Sociale: Systèmes Vivants, Invariance et Changement* (Paris: Editions Anthropos).

Barry, Tom *et al.* (1984) *The Other Side of Paradise: Foreign Control in the Caribbean* (New York: Grove Press).

Becker, Gary S. (1976) *The Economic Approach to Human Behavior* (Chicago: The University of Chicago Press).

Beckford, George L. (1972) *Persistent Poverty* (New York: Oxford University Press).

Bensman, Joseph and Bernard Rosenberg (1963) *Mass, Class and Bureaucracy: The Evolution of Contemporary Society* (Englewood Cliffs, N.J.: Prentice-Hall, Inc).

Benoist, Jean (1968) *Types de Plantations et Groupes Sociaux à la Martinique* (Montréal: Centre de Recherches Caraïbes, Université de Montréal).

Black, Jan Knippers (1986) *The Dominican Republic: Politics and Development in an Unsovereign State* (Boston: Allen and Unwin).

Bouliane, Pierre (1979) *Volga Plage: Un Bidonville de Propriétaires.* Thèse de Maitrise, Département d'Anthropologie, Université de Montréal.

Bourdieu, Pierre et Jean Passeron (1970) *La Reproduction: Eléments Pour une Théorie du Système d'Enseignement* (Paris: Les Editions de Minuit).

Bourdieu, Pierre (1971) 'Reproduction Culturelle et Reproduction Sociale', in *Information Sur les Sciences Sociales*, 10(2), pp. 45–79.

Brereton, Bridget (1979) *Race Relations in Colonial Trinidad 1870–1900* (Cambridge: Cambridge University Press).

Brodber, Erna (1975) *A Study of Yards in the City of Kingston* (Kingston: Institute of Social and Economic Research, University of the West Indies, Mona Jamaica [Working Papers, No. 9]).

Bryce-Laporte, Roy Simon (1968) 'Family Adaptation of Relocated Slum Dwellers in Puerto Rico: Implications For Urban Research and Development' in *The Journal of Developing Areas*, 2, pp. 533–40.

Butterworth, Douglas S. (1980) *The People of Buena Ventura. Relocation of Slum Dwellers in Postrevolutionary Cuba* (Urbana: University of Illinois Press).

Chauleau, Liliane (1966) *La Société à la Martinique au XVIIe Siècle (1635–1713)* (Caen: Imprimerie Ozanne et Cie).

Chin, Myron W. (1978) 'Lower Cost Housing in the West Indies – Some Solutions', in Fahd H. Dakhil et al. (eds), *Housing Problems in Developing Countries* (New York: University of Petroleum and Minerals and John Wiley and Sons) pp. 115–23.

Clarke, Colin G. (1975) *Kingston, Jamaica: Urban Growth and Social Change, 1692–1962* (Berkeley: University of California Press).

Cope, Thomas and Donald V. Kurtz (1980) 'Default and the Tanda: A Model Regarding Recruitment for Rotating Credit Associations' in *Ethnology*, 19, pp. 213–31.

Corvington, George, Jr (1975) *Port-au-Prince au Cours des Ans. La Métropole Haitienne du XIXe Siècle 1804–1888* (Port-au-Prince: Henri Deschamps) vol. 3.

Cross, Malcolm (1979) *Urbanization and Urban Growth in the Caribbean* (New York: Cambridge University Press).

De Albuquerque, Klaus, et al (1980) 'Uncontrolled Urbanization in the Developing World: A Jamaican Case Study', in *Journal of Developing Areas*, 14(3), pp. 361–86.

Demogeot, C. et J. Roger (1976) *Bilan de Trois Années d'Expertises Criminelles en Martinique* (Fort-de-France: Centre d'Etudes et de Recherches Criminologiques, Centre Universitaire Antilles-Guyane).

Demorizi, Emilio Rodriguez (1978) *El Pleito Ovando-Tapia. Comienzos de la Vida Urbana en America* (Santo Domingo: Editora Del Caribe).

Deschamps Chapeaux, Pedro (1969) 'Cimarrones Urbanos' in *Revista de la Biblioteca Nacional Jose Marti*, 60(2) (mayo-junio) pp. 145–64.

Dickinson, James and Bob Russell (eds) (1986) *Family, Economy and State: The Social Reproduction Process Under Capitalism* (London: Croom Helm).

Doran, Michael E. and Renée A. Landis (1980) 'Origin and Persistence of an Inner-city Slum in Nassau', in *Geographical Review*, 70(2), pp. 182–93.

Duarte, Isis (1976) 'Condiciones Sociales del Servicio Domestico en la Republica Dominicana', in *Realidad Contemporanea*, 1 (3–4) (Diciembre) pp. 79–104.

Dubreuil, Guy (1965) 'La Famille Martiniquaise: Analyse et Dynamique', in *Anthropologica*, 7(3), pp. 103–29.

Eckstein, Susan (1977a) *The Poverty of Revolution: The State and the Urban Poor in Mexico* (Princeton: Princeton University Press).

Eckstein Susan, (1977b) 'The Debourgeoisement of Cuban Cities' in Irving

Louis Horowitz, (ed), *Cuban Communism* (New Brunswick: Transactions Books) pp. 119–40.

Elizabeth, Léo (1977) 'Le Passé', in Guy Lasserre et al., *Atlas des Départements Français D'Outre-mer: La Martinique* (Bordeaux: Centre D'Etudes de Géographie Tropicale du CNRS) pp. 1–4.

Everitt, John C. (1985) 'The Growth and Development of Belize City', in *Journal of Latin American Studies*, 18, pp. 75–112.

Eyre, L. Alan (1972) 'The Shantytowns of Montego Bay, Jamaica', in *Geographical Review*, 62(3), pp. 394–413.

Eyre, L. Alan (1984) 'The Internal Dynamics of Shantytowns in Jamaica', in *Caribbean Geography*, 1(4), pp. 256–71.

Fass, Simon M. (1978) *Families in Port-au-Prince: A Study of the Economics of Survival* (Ph.D. dissertation, University of California at Los Angeles).

Fass, Simon M. (1980) *The Economics of Survival: A Study of Poverty and Planning in Haiti* (Washington, DC: Agency for International Development).

Fontaine, Pierre Michel (ed.) (1986) *Race, Class and Power in Brazil* (Los Angeles: Center for Afro-American Studies, University of California).

Franger, Ulrich (1978) 'Urban Policy Implementation in the Dominican Republic, Jamaica, and Puerto Rico', in *Ekistics*, 45(226).

Frazier, E. Franklin (1939) *The Negro Family in the United States* (Chicago: University of Chicago Press).

Fried, Morton H. (1956) 'Some Observations on the Chinese in British Guiana', in *Social and Economic Studies*, 5(1), pp. 54–73.

Gans, Herbert J. (1972) 'The Positive Functions of Poverty', in *American Journal of Sociology*, 78(2), pp. 275–89.

Geertz, Clifford (1962) 'The Rotating Association: A "Middle Rung" in Development', in *Economic Development and Cultural Change*, 10, pp. 241–63.

Genteuil, Yves (1977) 'Fort-de-France', in Guy Lasserre et al., *Atlas des Départements Français D'Outre-Mer: La Martinique* (Bordeaux: Centre d'Etudes de Géographie Tropicale du CNRS) pp. 1–2.

Gilbert, Neil (1970) *Clients or Constituents* (San Francisco: Jossey-Bass, Inc.).

Glondu, Patrice (1983) *Le grand Marché de Fort-de-France: Etude d'un Marché en Faux* (Talence: Université de Bordeaux III, Institut de Géographie).

Godelier, Maurice (1982) 'The Problem of the Reproduction of Socio-Economic Systems: A New Epistemological Context', in Ino Rossi (ed.), *Rural Sociology* (New York: Columbia University Press) pp. 259–91.

Goodenough, Stephanie (1978) 'Race, Status and Ecology in Port-de-Spain, Trinidad', in Colin G. Clarke (ed.), *Caribbean Social Relations* (Liverpool: Centre for Latin American Studies, University of Liverpool) pp. 17–45.

Goudet, Françoise (1973) *Le Quartier de L'Assainissement à Pointe-à-Pitre (Guadeloupe). Contribution à L'Etude des Phénomènes de Croissance et de Rénovation Urbaines en Milieu Tropical* (Talence: Centre D'Etudes de Géographie Tropicale, Domaine Universitaire de Bordeaux).

Gugler, Joseph (1980) 'A Minimum of Urbanism and a Maximum of Ruralism: The Cuban Experience', in *International Journal of Urban and Regional Research*, 4(4), pp. 516–35.

Hall, N. A. T. (1983) 'Slavery in Three West Indian Towns: Christiansted,

Fredericksted and Charlotte Amalie in the late Eighteenth and Early Nineteenth Century', in B. W. Higman (ed.), *Trade, Government and Society in Caribbean History 1700–1920* (Kingston: Heinemann Educational Books) pp. 17–38.

Hawkins, C. J. (1973) *Theory of the Firm* (London: Macmillan).

Hazard, Samuel (1871) *Cuba with Pen and Pencil* (Hartford, Conn.: Hartford Publishing Company).

Hearn, Lafcadio (1923) *Two Years in the French West Indies* (New York: Harper and Brothers Publishers).

Herskovits, Melville J. (1941) *The Myth of the Negro Past* (New York: Harper).

Herskovits, Melville, Jean and Frances (1947) *Trinidad Village* (New York: Octagon Books).

Hope, Kempe Ronald (1986) *Urbanization in the Commonwealth Caribbean* (Boulder: Westview Press).

Horowitz, Michael M. (1967) *Morne-Paysan: Peasant Village in Martinique* (New York: Holt, Rinehart and Winston).

Hudson, Brian J. (1980) 'Urbanization and Planning in the West Indies', in *Caribbean Quarterly*, 26(3), pp. 1–17.

Humbert, Amédée (1975) *Genèse, Historique et Evolution des Quartiers d'Habitat Spontané: Etude Concernant le Quartier 'Volga Plage' à Fort-de-France* (Fort-de-France: Mairie de la Ville de Fort-de-France [Miméo]).

Hurbon, Laënnec (1983) 'Racisme et Sous-Produit du Racisme: Immigrés Haitiens et Dominicains en Guadeloupe', in *Les Temps Modernes*, 33 (441–2), pp. 1988–2003.

INSEE (Institut National de la Statistique et des Etudes Economiques) (1983) *Résultats du Recensement de la Population dans les Départements d'Outre-Mer: Martinique* (Schoelcher: INSEE).

INSEE (Unpublished) *Enquête Budget de Famille Antilles-Guyane 1984– 1985. Dossier de Sainte Thérèse* (Martinique: INSEE).

Janin, J. (1924) *La Ville et la Paroisse de Fort-de-France* (Avignon: Aubanel).

Jelin, Elizabeth (1977) 'Migration and Labor Force Participation of Latin American Women: The Domestic Workers in the Cities', in *Signs*, 3(1) (Autumn) pp. 129–41.

Johnson, Howard (1987) 'The Chinese in Trinidad in the Late Nineteenth Century', in *Ethnic and Racial Studies*, 10(1), pp. 82–95.

Joyau, Auguste (1967) *La Martinique: Carrefour du Monde Caraïbe* (Fort-de-France: Editions des Horizons Caraïbes).

Katzin, Margareth F. (1959) 'Partners: An Informal Savings Institution in Jamaica', in *Social and Economic Studies*, 8, pp. 436–40.

Katzman, David M. (1978) *Seven Days a Week: Women and Domestic Service in Industrializing America* (New York: Oxford University Press).

Kearns, K. C. (1973) 'Belmopan: Perspective on a New Capital', in *Geographical Review*, 63, pp. 147–69.

Kovats-Beaudoux, Edith (1969) *Une Minorité Dominante: Les Blc ·cs Créoles de la Martinique*. Ph.D. dissertation, University of Paris.

Kurtz, Donald E. (1973) 'The Rotating Credit Association: An Adaptation to Poverty', in *Human Organization*, 32, pp. 49–58.

Labat, J. B. (1724) *Nouveau Voyage aux Iles de l'Amérique* (La Haye: P. Husson, T. Johnson, P. Gosse et Cie) vol. II.

Labetan, Richard (1982) *Sainvillias-Sainvilliens* (Fort-de-France: Imprimerie Désormeaux).

LaGuerre, John Gaffar (ed.) (1974) *Calcutta to Caroni: The East Indians of Trinidad* (Trinidad: Longman Caribbean Ltd).

Laguerre, Michel S. (1978) 'Ticouloute and His Kinfolk: The Study of a Haitian Extended Family', in Demitri B. Shimkin et al (eds), *The Extended Family in Black Societies* (The Hague: Mouton) pp. 406–45.

Laguerre, Michel S. (1982) *Urban Life in the Caribbean* (Cambridge: Schenkman Publishing Co.).

Laguerre, Michel S. (1987) 'Migration and Urbanization in Haiti', in *Sociologus*. 37(2), pp. 118–39.

Laitinen, Kenneth (1980) *A Theory of the Multi-Product Firm* (New York: North-Holland Publishing Co.).

Lanz, Gregorio (1969) 'Servicio Domestico: Una Esclavitud?', in *Estudios Sociales*, 11(4) (Diciembre) pp. 197–207.

LeBouc, B. (1976) *Regards sur la Criminalité à Fort-de-France* (Fort-de-France: Centre d'Etudes et de Recherches Criminologiques, Centre Universitaire Antilles-Guyane).

Lefebvre, Henri (1976) *The Survival of Capitalism: Reproduction of the Relations of Production* (New York: St Martin's Press).

Letchimy, Serge (1984a) *Urbanisme et Urbanisation à la Martinique: Le Cas de Fort-de-France*. Thèse de Doctorat de 3eme Cycle, Institut de Géographie, Université de Paris, Paris IV (Sorbonne), 2 vols.

Letchimy, Serge (1984b) Traditions et Créativité: Les Mangroves Urbaines de Fort-de-France. *Carbet, Revue Martiniquaise de Sciences Sociales*, 2, pp. 83–101.

Letchimy, Serge (1985) 'La Restructuration et la Réhabilitation du Quartier Texaco à Fort-de-France. Les Dossiers de l'Outre-Mer', in *Bulletin d'Information du CENADDOM*, 78–9, pp. 126–34.

Levy, Joseph J. (1976) *Un Village du Bout du Monde. Modernisation et Structures Villageoises aux Antilles Françaises* (Montréal: Les Presses de L'Université de Montréal).

Lewis, Oscar (1961) *Children of Sanchez* (New York: Random House).

Lewis, Oscar (1966) *La Vida: A Puerto Rican Family in the Culture of Poverty: San Juan and New York* (New York: Random House).

Light, Ivan H. (1972) *Ethnic Enterprise in America: Business and Welfare Among Chinese, Japanese and Blacks* (Berkeley: University of California Press).

Lindsay, Forbes (1911) *Cuba and Her People of Today* (Boston: L. C. Page and Company).

Lipton, Michael (1977) *Why Poor People Stay Poor: Urban Bias in World Development* (Cambridge, Mass.: Harvard University Press).

Loon, Paul van (1983) *A Dynamic Theory of the Firm: Production, Finance and Investment* (New York: Springer-Verlag).

Malefijt, Annemarie de W..al (1963) *The Javanese of Surinam: Segment of a Plural Society* (Assen: Van Gorcum).

Marieu, Jean (1977) 'Population', in Guy Lassere et al., *Atlas des*

Départements Français D'Outre-Mer: La Martinique (Bordeaux: Centre d'Etudes de Géographie Tropicale du CNRS) pp. 1–8.

Martin-Fugier, Anne (1979) *La Place des Bonnes* (Paris: Bernard Grasset).

Marx, Karl (1847) *The Poverty of Philosophy* (New York: International Publishers).

Marx, Karl (1936) *Capital: A Critique of Political Economy* (New York: The Modern Library).

Mathews, Thomas G. (1980) 'African Presence in XVII Century Puerto Rican Religious Ceremonies', in S. Jeffrey K. Wilkerson (ed), *Cultural Traditions and Caribbean Identity: The Question of Patrimony* (Gainesville: Center for Latin American Studies, University of Florida) pp. 157–71.

McClelland, D. C. (1961) *The Achieving Society* (Princeton, N.J.: Van Nostrand).

Mémoire Contenant l'Avis du Seigneur de Boulaye au Sujet de l'Établissement d'une Ville au Fort Royal, 5 avril 1700. Arch. DOM/TOM No. 101.

Mémoire sur le Fort Royal, Rochemore, 15 Octobre 1761. Arch. DOM/TOM.

Mémoire Historique, Descriptif et Militaire sur le Fort Royal, Moreau de Jones, 18 Février 1816. Arch. DOM/TOM No. 518 bis.

Miles, William F. S. (1986) *Elections and Ethnicity in French Martinique* (New York: Praeger).

Mincer, Jacob and Solomon Polachek (1974) 'Family Investments in Human Capital: Earnings of Women', in Theodore W. Schultz (ed.), *Economics of the Family* (Chicago: The University of Chicago Press) pp. 397–429.

Nett, Emily M. (1966) 'The Worker Class in a Developing Country: Ecuador', in *Journal of Inter-American Studies*, 8(3) (Summer) pp. 437–52.

Norvell, Douglas G. and James S. Wehrly (1969) 'A Rotating Credit Association in the Dominican Republic', in *Caribbean Studies*, 9(1), pp. 45–52.

Orlando Haza, Luis (1972) 'Urban Growth in the Dominican Republic: A Descriptive Overview', in Gustavo A. Antonini (ed.), *Public Policy and Urbanization in the Dominican Republic* (Gainesville: Center for Latin American Studies, University of Florida) pp. 23–54.

Pamphile, Joël (1985a) 'Une Cour Urbaine: La Cour Constantin', in *La Mouina*, 5, pp. 6–7.

Pamphile, Joël (1985b) 'Quelques Aspects de la Construction Spontanée à la Martinique. Les Dossiers de L'Outre-Mer', in *Bulletin d'Information du CENADDOM*, 78–9, pp. 74–9.

Paquette, Romain (1969) 'Divergences de Politique en Matière d'Habitation Populaire Dans les Villes Antillaises: Une Ville Française et Une Ville Anglaise', in *La Revue de Géographie de Montréal*, 23(2), pp. 123–36.

Pareek, Udai (1970) 'Poverty and Motivation', in Vernon L. Allen (ed.), *Psychological Factors in Poverty* (Chicago: Markham Publishing Co.) pp. 300–17.

Peet, Richard (1975) 'Inequality and Poverty: A Marxist-Geographic Theory', in *Annals of the Association of American Geographers*, 65(4), pp. 564–71.

Petit-Mau (1947) *La Cour Clindor* (Martinique: Imprimerie Renaissance).

Petitjean-Roget, Bernard (1983) 'Pour Comprendre la Situation Economique des Antilles', in *Les Temps Modernes*, 39(441–2), 1852–71.

Perrson, Gunnar (1978) *Essays on Mobility and Social Reproduction* (Stockholm: Arkiv Avhandlingsserie).

Portes, Alejandro and D. Frances Ferguson (1975) *Comparative Ideologies of Poverty: Latin America and the United States* (Los Angeles: School of Architecture and Urban Planning, University of California).

Potter, Robert B. (1981) 'Industrial Development and Urban Planning in Barbados', in *Geography*, 292(66), pp. 225–8.

Potter, Robert B. (1983) 'Urban Development, Planning and Demographic Change 1970–80 in Barbados', in *Caribbean Geography*, 1, pp. 3–12.

Proudhon, Pierre Joseph (1888) *The Philosophy of Misery* (Boston: Benj. R. Tucker).

Réaud, Guilène (1977) 'Commerce', in Guy Lassere et al., *Atlas des Départements Français D'Outre-Mer: La Martinique* (Bordeaux: Centre d'Etudes de Géographie Tropicale du CNRS) pp. 1–2.

Reid, Margaret G. (1934) *Economics of Household Production* (New York: Wiley).

Reid, Margaret G. (1974) 'Comment', in Theodore W. Schultz (ed.), *Economics of the Family* (Chicago: The University of Chicago Press) pp. 157–9.

Relouzat, C. (1968) *Fort-de-France: Sa Naissance, Sa vie* (Fort-de-France: Librairie Relouzat).

Revert, Eugène (1949) *La Martinique* (Paris: Nouvelles Editions Latines).

Rollins, Judith (1985) *Between Women: Domestics and Their Employers* (Philadelphia: Temple University Press).

Sable, Victor (1955) *La Transformation des isles d'Amérique en Départements Français* (Paris: Editions Larose).

Safa, Helen I (1974) *The Urban Poor of Puerto Rico* (New York: Holt, Rinehart and Winston).

Salmon, Lucy M. (1901) *Domestic Service* (London: Macmillan).

Sandbrook, Richard (1982) *The Politics of Basic Needs: Urban Aspects of Assaulting Poverty in Africa* (Toronto: University of Toronto Press).

Santos, Milton (1979) *The Shared Space: The Two Circuits of the Urban Economy in Underdeveloped Countries* (Methuen: London).

Sarbin, Theodore R. (1970) 'The Culture of Poverty, Social Identity, and Cognitive Outcomes', in Vernon L. Allen (ed.), *Psychological Factors in Poverty* (Chicago: Markham Publishing Co.) pp. 29–46.

Schultz, Theodore W. (1974) 'Fertility and Economic Values', in Theodore W. Schultz (ed.), *Economics of the Family* (Chicago: The University of Chicago Press) pp. 3–22.

Scott, George T. (1939) *Symposium on Household Employment* (New York: Federal Council of Churches).

Sévère, Victor (1931) L'Urbanisme aux Colonies: Fort-de-France (1639–1931), *L'Architecture*, XLIV (8), pp. 275–88.

Shimkin, Demitri, et al. (1978) *The Extended Family in Black Societies* (The Hague: Mouton).

Slater, Mariam K. (1977) *The Caribbean Family. Legitimacy in Martinique* (New York: St Martin's Press).

Smith, Raymond T. (1956) *The Negro Family in British Guiana* (London: Routledge and Kegan Paul).

Smith, Raymond T. (1963) 'Culture and Social Structure in the Caribbean: Some Recent Work on Family and Kinship Studies', in *Comparative Studies in Society and History*, 6(1) (Winter) pp. 24–45.

Smith, Margo L. (1973) 'Domestic Service as a Channel of Upward Mobility for the Lower Class Woman: The Lima Case', in Ann Pescatello (ed.), *Female and Male in Latin America* (Pittsburg: University of Pittsburg Press). pp. 191–207.

Soen, Dan and Patrice De Comarond (1972) 'Savings Associations Among the Bamileke: Traditional and Modern Cooperation in Southwest Cameroon', in *American Anthropologist*, 74(5), pp. 1170–9.

Spiegel, Hans B. C. and Alexander R. H. Walling (1974) 'Decentralization: An Introductory Sketch', in Hans B. C. Spiegel (ed.), *Citizen Participation in Urban Development: Decentralization* (Fairfax, Virginia: Learning Resources Corporation) pp. 3–16.

Spilerman, Seymour and David Elesh (1971) 'Alternative Conceptions of Poverty and Their Implications for Income Maintenance', in *Social Problems*, 18, pp. 358–73.

Stack, Carol (1975) *All Our Kin: Strategies for Survival in a Black Community* (New York: Harper and Row).

Stinner, William F., Klaus de Albuquerque and Roy S. Bryce-Laporte (1982) *Return Migration and Remittances: Developing a Caribbean Perspective*, RIIES Occasional Papers No. 3 (Washington DC: Research Institute on Immigration and Ethnic Studies, Smithsonian Institution).

Suivant, Louis, Béatrix Mora and Alain Fazincani (1986) *Politique d'Intervention sur les Quartiers Insalubres de la Martinique 1980–1985: 12 Etudes de l'ADUAM, Bilan et Perspectives* (Fort-de-France: ADUAM).

Tanic, Max (1984) *Pour un Habitat Adapté*, Thèse de Docteur Ingénieur en Urbanisme (Paris: Ecole des Ponts et Chaussées).

Tanic, Max (1985) Modes d'habiter dans un Quartier Populaire de Fort-de-France: L'expérience Texaco. *Carbet, Revue Martiniquaise de Sciences Humaines*, 3, pp. 51–63.

Taylor, Pam (1976) *Women Domestic Servants 1919–1939* (Birmingham: Centre For Contemporary Cultural Studies, The University of Birmingham).

Thomas, Clive Y. (1984) *Plantations, Peasants and State* (Los Angeles: Center for Afro-American Studies, University of California at Los Angeles).

Thomas, Clive Y. (1988) *The Poor and the Powerless: Economic Policy and Change in the Caribbean* (New York: Monthly Review Press).

Thompson, Arthur A. (1973) *Economics of the Firm: Theory and Practice* (New Jersey: Prentice Hall, Inc.).

Valentine, Charles A. (1968) *Culture and Poverty* (Chicago: University of Chicago Press).

Vaugirard, Raphaël (1985) 'Les Opérations Ebauches de Logements en Martinique', in *Les Dossiers de L'Outre-Mer*, 2(78–9), pp. 190–4.

Velez-Ibanez, Carlos G. (1983) *Bonds of Mutual Trust: The Cultural Systems of Rotating Credit Associations Among Urban Mexicans and Chicanos* (New Brunswick: Rutgers University Press).

Vernet, Elie Louis (1935) *La Domesticité Chez Nous. Question Sociale Haitienne* (Port-au-Prince: Imprimerie du Collège Vertières).

Wachtel, Howard M. (1971) 'Looking at Poverty From a Radical Perspective', in *Review of Radical Political Economics*, 3(3), pp. 1–19.

Wayne, Jack (1986) 'The Function of Social Welfare in a Capitalist Economy', in James Dickinson and Bob Russell (eds), *Family, Economy and State: The Social Reproduction Process Under Capitalism* (London: Croom Helm) pp. 1–20.

Weber, Max (1966) *The Theory of Social and Economic Organization* (New York: The Free Press).

Williams, Philip L. (1978) *The Emergence of the Theory of the Firm: From Adam Smith to Alfred Marshall* (New York: St Martin's Press).

Willis, Robert J. (1974) 'Economic Theory of Fertility Behavior', in Theodore W. Schultz (ed.), *Economics of The Family* (Chicago: The University of Chicago Press) pp. 25–75.

World Bank (1983) *Haiti: Urban Development Project*, Staff Appraisal Report (Washington DC: World Bank).

Wu, David Y. H. (1974) 'To Kill Three Birds with One Stone: The Rotating Credit Associations of the Papua New Guinea Chinese', in *American Ethnologist*, 1, pp. 565–84.

Zandvoort, F. J. (1979) 'Slum Improvement Projects in Columbia and Jamaica', in *Habitat International*, 4(1–2), pp. 171–3.

Zobel, Joseph (1980) *Black Shack Alley* (Washington DC: Three Continents Press).

Index